BECOME A WRITER
A STEP BY STEP GUIDE

Ann Evans

Greenstream Publishing

Greenstream Publishing
12 Poplar Grove
Ryton on Dunsmore
Warwickshire
CV8 3QE
United Kingdom

www.greenstreampublishing.com

Published by Greenstream Publishing 2012

ISBN 978-1-907670-24-4

With grateful thanks to Rob Tysall of Tysall's Photography for the cover design.

Table of Contents

Introduction

Ann Evans is probably best known for her children's books, but she also writes romance and non-fiction with more than 1,000 articles published in a wide variety of magazines and newspapers. When working as a staff feature writer for *The Coventry Telegraph*, her animal rescue series, *Pet SOS* won the RSPCA Media Award.

However, Ann says that she certainly was not born a writer. She says it is a craft that she has learned slowly and gradually. The knowledge you will find in this step by step guide has taken her many years to amass. The amount of rejected manuscripts in the early days of her writing could have filled a wardrobe. Correction, *did* fill a wardrobe.

When she first caught the writing bug Ann discovered the pitfalls the hard way, through trial and error, through rejection, through learning from other more successful writers, by attending seminars and writers' workshops, by reading 'how to' books and listening to author talks. She also took a correspondence course with The London School of Writing in the 1980s, which she says was the best money she has ever spent. Gradually the rejections lessened and the acceptances flourished. More recently, after 12 novels and over 1,000 articles published Ann has added tutoring and mentoring to her list of activities.

This book, like her creative writing classes, takes a logical step by step approach to the craft of writing – exactly the same approach as Ann took herself. The difference being that everything is here within the covers of this book not spread far and wide over many years. Ann is confident that this guide will provide a basic foundation for anyone who wants to write as a hobby or even as a career.

However, there are no guarantees when it comes to writing. Even established authors cannot guarantee that their next book will sell or even be accepted. Stories for magazines and newspapers can be 'spiked' or rejected at the last minute. Having a degree in journalism will not guarantee you a place on a newspaper. However, understanding your craft, loving the written word, striving always to improve and knowing how and where to present your work will put you ahead of the rest.

Of course it is down to the individual as to how successful you are, but by following this guide and the exercise set at the end of each chapter you will gain the fundamental knowledge and know-how to write successfully to your heart's content.

To coin a terrible cliché which Ann will be reminding you *not* to use in your stories, if you want to build your ivory tower, you need to lay down solid foundations first. This book will allow you to do just that.

Chapter One:
Make time to write

Step 1: Getting Organised

Many people fail in their writing ambitions simply because they just cannot get organised and make the time to write. People lead such busy lives that they often feel guilty for wanting to sit down and write. They feel they ought to be working, doing the housework, decorating, gardening, cooking, taking care of the home and family and so on. The thing is, if you wait for all that to happen before you give yourself permission to indulge in your passion for writing, you will never start.

So just as you allot time for your normal activities, allocate some specific time every day to write. Even an hour a day is hugely beneficial. The trick is to write regularly. It will improve your skills, it will make you feel like you really are a writer, so that those around you will realise this too, and (hopefully) respect your ambitions.

Make time for yourself

Set yourself a specific time which is your writing time and stick to it. I can almost hear you cry that there are not enough hours in the day as it is. Then why not get up an hour earlier or go to bed an hour later? If you take a lunch-break at work, find a quiet place to sit – and write. Place notebooks and pens around the house so you can jot down thoughts and ideas as they occur to you. Keep a notepad by the side of the bed as the best ideas can jump into your head just as you are dropping off to sleep; or they come in dreams and nightmares. If you do not jot these thoughts straight down, they will disappear forever.

Once you have set aside a specific time just for writing, make that a priority, so when you sit down to write – write! Do not wait for inspiration – inspiration generally comes at the least opportune moment. Often you are feeling in a creative mood as you are carrying out everyday chores, so hold onto those thoughts until you can sit down at your notepad or keyboard.

If, as you sit, you find yourself unable to think of a word to write, then write the first thing that comes into your head, just to get your brain ticking over and your fingers tapping. Many times I have actually typed: *"I haven't a clue what to write, dum de dum, I thought I might write a mystery but...."* Before long you will find you are writing something that you will not want to delete, and you will be off and into the swing of writing again.

A handy exercise when you are absolutely stuck for something to write is to literally copy, word for word, full stop for full stop, a paragraph or two from a published book by an author whom you admire. This is such good practice for getting the 'feel' of the layout for your own writing. It brushes up on indenting paragraphs, and the correct way to punctuate around dialogue. And if you have chosen an admired scene, you will be able to follow briefly in that author's footsteps in writing the exact words and phrases that they chose. This is not to encourage you to try and emulate another author, simply an exercise that somehow releases your own inhibitions when crafting a scene. Try it and see.

So remember, make time to write – and write.

Find time to read

I suspect that you manage to find time to read your favourite magazines and novels. So why not add 'how-to' books on creative writing to your home library? Whether it is how to write magazine articles, how to write romantic fiction, how to write short stories, how to write for children – or whatever, these books are incredibly useful, informative and inspirational. Absorb as much information, knowledge and other writers' experiences as you can. Invest in a copy of *The Writers and Artists Yearbook,* and browse through that whenever you have a few minutes to spare. It will be time and money well spent.

When reading fictional novels, as well as enjoying the stories, also read with the aim of learning from them. Look at the use of vocabulary; the sentence structure; the dialogue. If a particular scene moved you to laughter or tears, or made the hairs on the back of your neck prickle, read it over again and see if you can analyse how the author created this effect.

Step 2: Tools of the trade

Notepad and pencil are your basics to begin with. Add to this a good dictionary and use it to check every word you are not sure off. Do not let mistakes slip through. By all means have a thesaurus but do not be a slave to it. Usually the first word that comes to mind is the natural one for your own individual style; if you are forever looking for a more unusual alternative, your writing could look 'forced' and unnatural.

You will eventually need a computer (or a friend with a computer) even if you do not like writing directly onto one. If you intend trying to get your work published then it will need to be printed or typed.

Additional items: More notebooks and pencils/pens. Place them around the house, in the car/garage/shed/greenhouse – everywhere that you spend time doing other things, because the best ideas occur when you least expect them. If you fail to jot them down they will vanish like the morning mist.

A log book: By this I mean a notebook in which you keep a record of everything you send out. Make columns showing: date sent; title of work; where it was sent; whether it was accepted or rejected; publication date; amount earned. Do not rely on memory especially when you are sending work out regularly. You need to keep a track of your stories and articles.

Handy stuff: An ideas notebook – one idea per page or double page. This allows you the space to jot down thoughts as to what you could do with this basic idea. Will it make a poem, maybe a short story, could it develop into an article or even a novel? Jot down all the possibilities for this idea; keep adding your thoughts to this page, and gradually it will become clear what the best way(s) of dealing with it would be. At a writers' conference I remember a non-fiction writer saying that from one idea (a particular cathedral) and subsequent research, he wrote and had published 72 different articles and stories.

More handy 'tools': An ideas box or folder. Keep cuttings, photographs and objects that have caught your eye. They might inspire a story or article.

Nice stuff: Buy a scrapbook to paste all your published cuttings in.

Useful things: Small recording device to record spur of the moment thoughts and interviews. Many mobile phones have a recording function. Also stock up on A4 envelopes, typing paper, plain postcards and stamps.

Words of Wisdom

"Find your own voice – your own style of writing. I spent a lot of time not getting on with the writing because of not knowing how to say what I wanted to in some kind of formal way. Then accepted that I needed to write as I speak so that I could be comfortable with what I was saying and so that it came across as really me speaking through the book. I didn't want to write a professional text – I wanted to connect with real people on an equal basis. Just as I had done in my professional practice."
Susan Jane Smith, B.Sc.

Exercise 1

List the hours in the day and the days in the week. Now slot in your activities and see when you have an hour or half an hour, or just ten minutes to devote to writing. Highlight these times in your diary and stick to them.

Exercise 2

Treat yourself to some 'tools of the trade'.

Exercise 3

Write a short piece about how you see yourself a few years into the future, having accomplished some of your writing ambitions or dreams. This exercise is purely for you, so write this as honestly as you can. Put into words what your writing ambitions really are.

Exercise 4

If you want to write for publication, take a look at the magazines on the newsagents' shelves, new books in bookshops and library books. Be aware of the many different genres and possibilities, and hone into the ones that particularly appeal to you.

Exercise 5

Select something that you have particular enjoyed reading, e.g. a book, a short story, a poem or article. Now, for the next five minutes – time yourself, write down what was particularly good about it.

Tip

Dreaming about being a writer is wasting your valuable time. The only way to become a writer is to write – and keep on writing.

Chapter Two:
What to Write

Step 3: Deciding what to write

You may hope one day to be a writer of blockbuster sagas; you may want to write columns for the women's pages of magazines; you might want to write technical articles for trade magazines; or maybe your intention is to write for radio or television. The world is your oyster but my advice is to start small and work upwards, learning as you go. Do not run before you can walk.

If you start off writing something major but you have not yet mastered the basics, then you are letting yourself in for a lot of unnecessary re-writing. You will soon learn that writing is all about re-writing. You have to hone and polish your work relentlessly before you can be satisfied. So do not give yourself unnecessary extra work by making mistakes with the elementary principles to begin with. You need sound, solid foundations on which to build.

Basic rules of writing

To begin with, here are a few of the most fundamental rules to writing. There will be lots more to come. So whatever you are writing....

- Do not waste words: do not waffle or pad out unnecessarily.

- Ensure your spelling and punctuation are correct: there is no excuse for mistakes here. Be especially aware of getting punctuation around dialogue correct.

- Never write in stone: realise that your first draft is just that. Your work will improve with editing and polishing.

- Be correct with your facts: double check everything. If you submit work to an editor containing incorrect information that editor will not look too favourably on anything else you submit.

- Present your work as perfectly as you can: Writing for publication is a professional business, so be professional with your approach and your presentation.

If you can get into good practice whatever you write, these basics will become second nature, leaving you plenty of breathing space to be creative.

Step 4: Making a start

My advice to anyone just starting out on the road to becoming a writer, is
– as this book suggests, take it a step at a time. A good starting point is
writing a 'Letter to the Editor'.

Readers' Letters.

You might not consider writing a 'Letter to the Editor as actual creative
writing, but these letters are ideal starting points and where many a top
writer has begun their writing career. Letters to a magazine editor may be
short and to the point but they still require you, the author to come up
with an interesting topic; to craft the sentences skilfully; to write to the
style of the publication; and present it neatly and legibly.

Look on readers' letters as mini short stories or mini articles. On the
positive side, get a 'letter to the editor' published and you will see your
name in print; your thoughts and cleverly crafted words will be published;
you will be paid for your efforts; and it will not have taken up very much
of your time.

You only have to browse through the numerous magazines and
newspapers on the newsagents' shelves to see the wide range of
publications that have a readers' letters page. Some pay exceptionally
well, others just pay for the 'star' letter. Many like you to include a
photograph to illustrate your letter – for which they also pay.

Analyse those letters pages

Letters to magazines vary in length, style and content, so it is necessary to
analyse the sort of letter an individual magazine publishes. Do not assume
they are all the same. So, do a word count and keep within the limit. Look
at the content. Do they publish letters which comment on something that
the magazine has previously published? Are the letters on controversial
subjects? Are they humorous? Are they family orientated? Get to know
what different magazines like to publish.

As well as letters, some magazines publish 'tips'. For example a
gardening magazine might be interested to publish your tip on keeping
snails away from your lettuces. A lifestyle magazine might like to know
how to tell if an egg is still fresh. A motoring magazine might like to
know your tips on getting more mileage out of a litre of fuel.

Local newspapers and certain magazines publish reviews on plays, films,
books, games, CDs etc. Do your market research, contact the editor and
see if there is a slot for you. If you become a regular contributor to these
columns, even if you don't earn much in remuneration, you may make up

for it in freebies!

The very first thing I ever had published was a 'letter to the editor' at *Weekend Magazine* many moons ago. It earned me the fantastic sum of £1.50. I cut the letter out and pasted it in my scrapbook. It looked quite lost and lonely to begin with, but not for long.

This is the letter that launched my writing career…

My washing machine was broken, my kitchen floor flooded. My husband came to the rescue – he bought me a mop!

Oddly enough my husband was the subject of my next 'letter to the editor' too…

I feared romance had died when my husband replaced a photo of me on his dressing table with one of a motorbike!

It is surprising how you can turn many little incidents into 'readers letters', allow yourself some 'poetic licence' and turn a mundane incident into something entertaining.

How to write a 'Letter to the Editor'.

Select the magazine you want to try for. Read the magazine from cover to cover. Look at the advertisements and photographs, read the articles and stories and analyse the sort of person who would buy this magazine. Make sure your writing will appeal to that readership.

Analyse the letters:

- What is the minimum and maximum word length of the letters?
- Do any of the letters refer to something in a previous issue?
- Are any of the letters 'handy' tips?
- Are any of the letters amusing 'family/toddler' incidents?
- Are the letters controversial or opinion pieces?
- Are the letter comments about something in the news or on TV?
- Do the letters have accompanying photographs?
- Can you understand why the editor selected each of the letters he printed?

Once you get a 'feel' for the letters published in a particular journal, then try your hand at writing something that you believe would slide in very nicely and not look out of place on that page. So:

- Choose your topic.

- Write it as best as you can.

- Now re-read it. Ask yourself if it has a snappy opening sentence, or is it a long, unnecessary preamble? Have you made your point, or is it jumbled? Is it lively to read or dull? Is it within the word limit?

- Re-write it with a more critical eye. Make the opening sentence catchy. Work on the main 'story' so that it is clear. Take out or change dull phrases; make it snappy, lively and easy to read. Ensure it is within the word count.

- Re-write it again, making it word perfect. Read it aloud or get someone to read it aloud to you – and listen. If there is anything, however slight, that jars, then work on it until you are completely happy.

- If there is an option to include a relevant photograph, do so.

- Tips for taking photographs for magazines: Make the subject fill the frame so there is no unnecessary background. If you are sending it as a jpg, it should be 300dpi. In your letter, write a brief caption for the photograph.

- When sending your letter, be sure to include your name, address, phone number (even when sending by email).

- Jot the details down in your 'Log Book'.

How to write a reader's 'Handy Tip'.

As above, analyse the tips that have already been published, note the word length. Look to see if 'tips' are illustrated with a photograph?

- Choose your topic. You might have your own handy tip – ways you have been doing things all your life; or you might want to research the subject and come up with something brand new. Maybe you can think of some 'old wives tales' – the good old fashioned ways of doing things.

- Above all, look at the readership of the magazine and ensure your tip is appropriate to them.

- Write this up as best you can.

- Now re-read it bearing in mind all the points above. Is it snappy, clear and interesting? Can you include a photograph?

- Re-write and re-write until you are totally happy with it.

How to write a review

Newspapers and magazines publish reviews on all kinds of things: books, plays, films, DVDs, computer games, products, restaurants, food and drink, the list goes on. Obviously to write a review, you need to have sampled the product – which is a bonus in itself whether it's a trip to the theatre, playing a computer game, or trying out a brand of moisturising cream.

Before you can put yourself forward to a newspaper, magazine or website to do reviews, you need to be adept in writing them, so, practice. The next time you go to the theatre or a restaurant, or use a product, write about it, even though it may be just for yourself to begin with.

Be sure to include the facts. If it is a theatre play, give details of the theatre, the dates the play runs, the running time, who the director is, who the main actors are. Once you have the facts, write your review honestly – but never brutally. The pen is a powerful tool and it's not nice to smash a budding actor's dreams by scathing words.

Similarly for a book review, include the facts – the title, author, ISBN number, price, who published it. Then write your opinion of the book – you could even publish your review on sites such as Amazon. It is good practice for you and you could be doing the author a favour too.

Once you are confident that you can write a review, do your market research. Study your local newspaper and any local free newspapers, you might find a regular column that publishes reviews. Offer your services (with an example of your style). You may not get paid for your review, but you should get your name in print. You may get a regular slot and could even be rewarded with other products to review – which you generally get to keep.

Words of Wisdom

"A writer is a person who feels more at home on the page than anywhere else."

Roz Morris

Exercise 1

Choose a newspaper/magazine that publishes Readers' Letters and/or Readers' Tips.

Read the magazine from cover to cover, looking at the photographs and the advertisements to define who its main readership is.

Exercise 2

After reading this magazine, write a review about it.

Exercise 3

Write a 'reader's letter' or a 'reader's tip' to the relevant letters page of this magazine, following all the advice given above. Put it aside for a few days.

Exercise 4

Write up another letter or tip in the meantime.

Exercise 5

Read through your original letter, and see if you can improve upon it in any way. If you are totally happy with it, send it off. Remember to jot down in your log book what the letter was about, where you sent it and the date. Good luck!

Tip

Is there a writers group near you that you could join? If not, why not try and start one with some like-minded friends?

Chapter Three:
Choosing a Genre

Step 5: Know what you are writing

You need to have a clear idea in your head as to what you are writing – and who your audience is. So ask yourself whether you are writing a short story, an article, a filler, the beginning of a novel, a radio story, a children's story – if so, what age range/ability? If it is an article, what is your purpose in writing it? Is it to entertain, enlighten, educate, amuse, shock, inform? If it is a short story is it for radio or for a magazine? If it is for radio, will it fit into an established time slot? If it is for a magazine, will the word length, style and content suit your targeted magazine?

If you have a clear idea what it is you are writing, and who your intended readership will be, it will help you to focus on producing a good piece of work.

Letters to the readers' page of a magazine are probably the only submission that can look 'amateurish' as these letters are supposed to have come from readers. Nevertheless, they should be legible, concise and have something to say which is relevant to that particular magazine.

All other contributions to magazines, newspapers, radio, TV, competitions etc., should look professional. Your work should be typed and double spaced. Pages should be numbered, with a word of the title and your name in the top corner. For example, page seven of my book *A Tropical Affair* would appear like this: *Tropical/Evans/7*

Include a brief covering letter simply saying what you are sending and if relevant, your 'credentials' as to why you are 'qualified' to write this piece (mainly for technical articles); and a neat title page giving the title of the work, number of words and your contact details. If you are sending your work by post rather than email, and you would like it back if they cannot use it, include return postage (SAE).

A short item such as a letter or filler, will take a fraction of the time it would take to write a novel, short story or article. But to see your written work and your name in a publication is a huge thrill – and a reason to be proud of yourself. You will be a published writer and there will be no stopping you.

My advice is that you should become accomplished in writing short pieces of work before diving into writing a TV drama or a block-busting novel. If you concentrate on writing shorter pieces of work to begin with, you will really get into the swing of writing well and being focused on what exactly you are doing and why – which is all good practice for the future. Also writing shorter pieces to begin with will highlight any areas of grammar, punctuation, presentation etc., that need to be perfected before you embark on something more time consuming such as a story or novel. The last thing you want is to be making the same basic mistakes over and over again.

Even if you are only writing for yourself or drafting out an idea, try and think professionally from the start. Never let spelling and punctuation mistakes pass you by. Make it second nature to rectify errors as you see them.

If you prefer writing your early drafts onto notepaper rather than a computer, it is a good idea to write on every other line, or every third line. That way you can make changes without getting too crowded out.

The Market Place

There are plenty of opportunities to write short pieces – or fillers for magazines. You only have to browse the newsagents to see the variety of magazines on offer. This is just the tip of the iceberg. *The Writers and Artists Yearbook* lists hundreds of publications; *Willings Press Guide* has even more and includes many trade and specialist magazines. There are also countless online magazines. All of these magazines need their pages filled with articles, stories, letters, tips and fillers. Many magazines offer contributor's guidelines. Look on their websites, you might be able to download them, or send a letter requesting them.

Market Research

Make sure you do your market research. Skipping this stage can result in you not getting your work published. Perfectly good articles and stories sometimes get rejected simply because the author has not done their market research well enough and has sent their work to an unsuitable publication or not allowed enough time for topical and time-sensitive pieces to be published. Monthly magazines usually work three months ahead. Weekly and daily papers also work well in advance for features and articles.

People read magazines for a variety of reasons. It might be for entertainment and relaxation; or to keep abreast of what is going on in their spheres of interest; or to be enlightened and educated in the subject. In fact for any number of reasons, but in a nutshell, people buy a specific magazine because they are interested in its content. So it is up to you to provide that magazine with something that will interest its readers.

You can work out the type of readership by looking at the content, its style, the adverts and illustrations. Target your work accordingly. If you do not do your market research you will not know what that magazine publishes, so you will not know what it wants.

If you already read certain magazines regularly you will know what that publication wants. You will also know what sort of person reads it, and the style/content of the stories/articles/fillers/letters within.

You cannot possibly look at all the magazines out there. So investing in a copy of *The Writers and Artists Yearbook* will be worth its weight in gold. Browse the newsagents' shelves to find writing magazines that appeal to you. If you happen to be sitting in the dentist or doctor's waiting room spend your time usefully by examining the magazines with a view to writing something for them.

Wherever possible, if you want to write for a particular magazine, read as many issues as you can get your hands on to get a 'feel' for it. Do not just guess at the sort of thing they publish.

Writing competitions:

Keep your eyes peeled for writing competitions too. Magazines run them, online writing sites run them – all kinds of organisations run them. Watch out for competition entry forms in libraries. Winning or being placed in a writing competition is a huge boost to a budding writer. But do not be downhearted if you do not win. You cannot actually know what will appeal to an individual judge or a panel of judges. However if you have your basics in order, they will not be marking you down on presentation. And if you write to your best ability and you are pleased with the finished result yourself, then chances are that someone else will like it too.

Step 6: Be professional

Writing for publication is a professional business. Your work has to stand up against submitted manuscripts from other professional writers, so give yourself the best possible chance by ensuring your presentation is as professional-looking as anything else the editor may have looked at that day. If you want editors to take you seriously, then your work, your presentation and your approach must be at a professional level.

Polish your work:

- Do not be satisfied with your first, second or third draft.

- Do not pad with unnecessary words.

- Do not try and impress with a long word when a short one would be better. On the other hand, do not use a short word if a long one is more appropriate.

- Ensure there are no punctuation, spelling or grammatical errors.

- If it is fiction, is the punctuation around the dialogue correct – and consistent?

- Be accurate. Are all your facts correct? Is your work trustworthy and reliable?

- Is it neatly typed? Are your pages numbered? Is it double spaced and if printed, is it printed on one side of A4 paper?

- Have you included a title page giving number of words and your contact details?

- Have you included a brief covering letter?

- Polish your work until it gleams.

Words of Wisdom

"Don't settle for the first idea you get, use it as a springboard for your story and tweak it, stretch it, play with it until you get something really strong and original".
Karen King

Exercise 1

Make a list of all the topics you know *something* about. Aim to reach around 30.

Exercise 2

Make a short-list of topics you are a bit of an expert at.

Exercise 3

Write up to 500 words on *one* of the topics from your list. Write it in whatever form you wish, e.g. an article, the beginnings of a short story, flash fiction, a poem – the choice is yours. Put this exercise aside for a day or two.

Exercise 4

Read your 500 word piece aloud. Be sure you read exactly what you have written – not what you *think* you have written. See if you can improve upon it.

Exercise 5

See if you can write similar pieces on some of your other topics.

Tip

Writing is like driving a car, once you've mastered the skill of driving, you can go anywhere. However, you wouldn't set out on a 100-mile trip before you'd even learnt how to change gear would you?

Chapter Four:
Getting out there

Step 7: Approaching an editor

Editors are (usually) quite human. They are not demonic monsters waiting to tear your manuscript – and you into shreds. Even so, it can be quite daunting when it comes to contacting them. The joy of email takes a lot of the fear away and is probably the best way of making contact when you have an idea to suggest or a finished manuscript to send.

Always try and send your enquiry letters or emails to the correct specific person. You can usually discover who this is by reading the magazine or studying the publisher's website.

Before approaching a magazine editor with an idea or the finished article remember they do not want to hear your life story or that you have slaved for five years in writing this masterpiece. They simply want your article/story, neatly presented and a polite, short covering letter asking if they can use it at their normal rates, plus your contact details. Then be brave, let your article go and allow it to stand up for itself.

If you are sending in a short story to a relevant magazine, unless specified, you do not usually have to send an enquiry letter first. Knowing the style and length they print should establish whether your story could be right for them or not.

Step 8: A need to know

Writers will often hear the advice – 'write about what you know'. But if you are restricted to writing about only what you know, most people's output would be fairly limited.

My advice is: if you don't know about a subject, find someone who does. Glean all the information you need from them along with other methods of research – until you really feel you know your subject. Then off you go – you will be writing about what you do know – even if it is only 'temporary'.

Afterwards, there is nothing wrong with asking the 'expert' who you interviewed if they would read through your article to make sure there are no glaring errors. In fact if they are being quoted, they will probably be delighted to have the opportunity to view their words to ensure they are not being misquoted. However, do not be coerced into changing your style to suit them. You are only asking them to check for incorrect or incomplete facts.

I remember one businessman I interviewed about his porcelain figurines, who wanted to see the finished article. I obliged. However, although there were no errors or anything incorrect with my article, he changed my phrasing so much that it became an advertisement for his product rather than an article.

I knew my editor would not accept it the way he wanted it and I told him so. However he insisted on having it his way leaving me with no choice but to refuse to put my name to it. The article never got submitted and the businessman did not get his product in the magazine. I had to stick to my guns as this was not advertising editorial that he was paying for. So hold onto your standards and be true to yourself.

Research

The things that writers write about cannot possibly come from inside their heads alone. Whether you are writing fiction or non-fiction, there will come a time when you need to research a subject.

These days, with the internet on hand, research could not be simpler. You can get an answer to practically anything simply by tapping in a few key words into a search engine on the internet. However, if you are using the internet for researching a subject that you intend to write about, take a good look at the source of your information. Make sure it is a reputable source and the facts are accurate. Double check your facts before you state them as true in your own writing. Do not rely on the internet alone. The library is an excellent and obvious source for research plus you might have your own personal collection of useful books. So the opportunities to do your research are all around.

Research can be fascinating. However you will find so much written, especially on the internet that it may slow you down in your writing. Or you will find so much information on your subject that you could get bamboozled and bogged down. You might feel that you have to get it all into your piece of writing – you do not .

Be selective, and also be careful not to simply transpose interesting snippets into your work just because they are interesting. Make sure it is relevant to what you are working on, and re-word your findings to merge in with your writing. Sometimes researched segments stand out like a sore thumb if they are just lifted and inserted into a story or article.

Books and the internet are great for gathering information, but additionally, you cannot beat talking to someone who really knows their subject. People generally like to chat about what they are interested in whether it is their work or hobby. So if you need to know something – ask an expert!

Interviewing someone may sound like a daunting prospect, and I would not suggest starting with a public figure or university lecturer or the like until you are competent and comfortable with the whole interviewing scenario.

However, you may need to know what life was like in the days of your parents or grandparents, so an interview with a relative, friend or an elderly person might be necessary. Or maybe a character in your story is in a profession that you need to know about if your story is to be believable.

Another good reason for 'asking an expert' is that in non-fiction articles particularly, including personal quotes will really bring your article to life.

So if there is a 'need to know' do not let it hold you back. The answers are out there just waiting for you to find them.

Step 9: The Interview

The best way to find out anything is to talk to an expert in the subject, and if you can develop a good interviewing technique, then you will be able to gather all the information you need for your story or article. However, good interviewing skills need working on so that you can set your interviewee at ease and get them talking. Here are some tips on how to go about this:

Preparing for your interview

You need to know in advance what information you need. So write your list of questions (in a logical sequence) with the first one crafted to put the interviewee at their ease. Be prepared however for the interviewee to surprise you with all kinds of information that you never expected – which often makes for an even better interview. So although you have worked out your list of questions, do not expect to stick to the list, and never recite them 'parrot fashion' oblivious to the person's answers.

If you are concentrating on the interviewee more questions will spring from their replies so be sure your questions are open-ended. The last thing you want is 'yes' and 'no' answers. Also gauge how much time you will need for your interview, maybe ten minutes, half an hour, longer? An hour and a half is probably the limit.

Recording the interview

Decide how you are going to record the interview. Shorthand is a brilliant way of recording interviews so if you did Pitman's shorthand or Teeline shorthand at college or work, I suggest you brush up on it. Otherwise invest in a small recording device – but practice using it beforehand, also make notes as you go. Personally, I take notes in shorthand. It is a skill that took me three years to learn (home study). However, I am reliably informed that Teeline shorthand can be learned a whole lot quicker. So give this some consideration because if you can master the skill of shorthand you will never look back.

If you are using a recording device however, and/or you have your own speed writing techniques, practice reading back from your notebook or recorder, it can be trickier than you might think.

I have used a Dictaphone twice in my interviewing career – the first time I pressed the 'pause' button while the interviewee and I had a cup of tea. Sadly, I forgot to press 'play' when the interview got under way, hence not a single word of the interview was recorded. My second disastrous interview took place outdoors on a blustery day and all I got was the sound of the wind gusting over the microphone. So practice using your recording techniques before tackling your first interview.

Never be afraid to ask the person you are interviewing to spell any words that you are not familiar with and always check the spelling of names.

Setting up the interview

Make the initial contact with the person or organisation, either through an email, letter or telephone call. Explain briefly who you are; what you are writing; whether you are hoping to get it published; and what you would like to interview them about. If they do not want to co-operate, simply respect that, thank them for their time and leave it. Look for someone else.

If they are agreeable, they might say they are free to talk that moment – so you will be glad you are well and truly prepared, as suggested earlier won't you? Alternatively, they might suggest a time when they will phone you/or you phone them for a telephone interview. In which case stick to the arranged date/time. They might ask you to send questions through on an email. Make sure you phrase your questions so they cannot answer a simple yes or no.

They might suggest you meet up. Obviously be sensible about this and if you are meeting for a coffee it is only polite to buy them the coffee as they are doing you the favour. Ask them if they mind you using a recorder. Some people do not like the idea of their every word being recorded. So be prepared with notebook and pencils in case they refuse. Even if you are recording the interview, make notes throughout in case your recorder fails – or you still have the 'pause' button pressed.

The interview

The only way to gather information from someone you are interviewing is to LISTEN.

Remember an interview is not a normal conversation when both parties contribute fairly equal amounts of conversation. Although you want your interview to come across as a chatty friendly conversation, in fact you will be listening a lot more than you will be talking. Your input will be to keep the conversation flowing by asking questions; following on from their comments with further questions – which you may not necessarily have planned.

Do's and Do Nots:

- **Do not** finish sentences for your interviewee.

- **Do not** be reminded of when something similar happened to you – and your interviewee ends up listening to your story.

- **Do not** disagree with their views. (Not out loud at any rate.)

- **Do not** wander too far off the subject.

- **Do** try to nod in agreement rather than verbally agreeing (unless it is a telephone interview) if you are using a recording device, or your continual 'yesses' may obliterate what they are saying.

- **Do** listen carefully and manipulate your questions to follow on from what they have said, rather than reeling your questions off parrot fashion.

- **Do** look interested.

- **Do** recognise when the interview is reaching its conclusion, and do not drag it out unnecessarily.

- **Do** thank them sincerely for giving up their time to talk to you.

After the interview

Write up your interview in *draft* form at the earliest possible opportunity. Write up notes, transcribe the recording. Also write up your observations about the interviewee, the surroundings, even how you felt about talking to this person. You might not use everything, but it will be in your first draft should you need it.

If an opening sentence springs to mind, write that down instantly, as often, once you get the opening line, the rest will flow.

Also be aware that sometimes the concluding sentence your interviewee says will be something quite profound. Maybe its human nature, but we sometimes subconsciously round things up with a concluding remark that says it all. In my experience it is usually just after you have put the top back on your pen and your notepad back in your bag.

Finally, celebrate your hard work and achievement with a chocolate biscuit and a cup of tea – or something stronger.

Words of Wisdom

"Learn the basic techniques of music and your writing will already be several steps ahead of the game. Whether it's rhythm, the movement between tempos, breaking a chord down into its constituent notes using arpeggio, or learning how long a pause needs to be, you will find spending just a little time with music opens up a whole store just filled with new boxes of tricks."
Dan Holloway.

Exercise 1

Practising on a friend or family member, interview them on a recent achievement or activity. Be sure you go through all the steps above in preparing for the interview.

Exercise 2

Conduct your interview, as outlined above.

Exercise 3

Write your interview up as an article or part of an article.

Exercise 4

Put this aside for a day or two. Then re-read it with a critical eye looking for ways of improving it.

Exercise 5

Select a magazine of your choice and a story, article, filler or letter that appeals to you and see if you can 'mirror' it with an idea of your own.

Tip

Interviewing and non-fiction writing can take you to amazing places and allow you to speak to fascinating people whom you wouldn't normally come into contact with. This line of writing can open doors!

Chapter Five:
Writing magazine articles

Step 10: Article Writing

I am a big fan of writing magazine articles. I must have written and had published well over 1,000 articles on every kind of subject imaginable. Two articles from opposite ends of the scale which spring to mind being an article on a Russian T-55 tank which was published in an 'off road' magazine and an article on brain surgery written when I was a feature writer for my local newspaper, the *Coventry Telegraph*. Two articles which are worlds apart on topics I had little knowledge of – until I had to write about them.

Writing articles has taken me to different countries and behind the scenes in all kinds of organisations. I have met the most interesting people and a fair few celebrities. I have experienced a flight in an army helicopter as they practised combat training; I have been on a police launch out in the Thames Estuary as they boarded an ocean going vessel while it was still moving. I have been involved in a simulated mountain rescue in Switzerland and lots of other amazing adventures simply because I was writing an article on it. Believe me, when you are a non-fiction writer it can open up all kinds of amazing opportunities. And, if all goes well, you get paid for your finished piece of writing too.

Your expertise

Do not think that you need to be an expert in a million and one subjects. In the words of Gordon Wells in his book, *The Craft of Writing Articles* all you need is the ability to write, an enquiring mind and a professional approach. As the writer you need to be able to gather information and know how to be selective in this gathering process. You need to be interested in the subject – even if only temporarily. Your enquiring mind needs to ask the right questions of the right people, and once you have acquired all the knowledge from the experts, your skill as a writer has to then untangle it like a giant jigsaw and place all the pieces in the right order to make a perfect picture that anyone can understand and appreciate.

Be aware of what a magazine article or feature is however. It is not a school or college essay or an academic thesis; neither is it a technical report or a fictional story. Your magazine article is the telling of something that will interest a great number of people. Your style of writing should attract others to read it. Firstly, it needs to catch the editor's eye and interest him so much that he wants to publish it. It should be accurate, entertaining, informative and lively.

Magazine editors constantly need articles that are interesting, original and easy to read. However because something is 'easy to read' most definitely does not mean it is easy to write. In the words of one anonymous writer, *"Easy reading is damned hard writing."*

Knowing who to write for

When writing an article you need to bear in mind the reader, so select the market for your article with care. Try and work out why readers have bought that particular magazine and what you are telling them. It is no use writing a basic lightweight article to a specialist magazine, nor an in-depth technical feature for a general interest magazine. So think carefully about what you want to say in your writing, and be aware of who it will interest.

Payment for articles varies from one magazine to another. Usually you get paid by the number of words – but whatever you do, do not try to pad out your article to increase your fee. No editor wants an article packed with superfluous words. Some smaller magazines and on-line sites do not pay at all. Nevertheless, it is worth going for these markets at the start of your writing career. Many published writers have written for free. It is good for your morale and for your CV.

For me the best thing about writing articles is actually getting out there and researching the topic, meeting people involved in the subject, and spending time, briefly in their world, absorbing yourself in something that is brand new and different for you. People, places, activities, hobbies, pets, nature, wildlife... so much is going on all around you. When you see something that catches your eye, consider how you could write about it to show others about this interesting subject.

Step 11: Article Topic

The usual advice is to write about what you know – which is definitely good advice. But I would also add, write about what interests you – even if you know nothing about the subject (as yet). If it has caught your attention, chances are it will interest others too. It pays to be as interested in as many things as possible.

The human element is vital to a good article too. Most people are interested in people, so an article just filled with dry factual information will simply be dry and factual. Bring it to life by writing about the people connected to your topic.

Keep an 'ideas notebook' to jot ideas down as they occur to you. Otherwise they will undoubtedly drift away. Note each idea down on a separate page, and then add other thoughts and off-shoots as to how you could use the basic idea, along with magazine titles which could be possible markets. Think of all the different angles associated with this one topic. Keep building up your 'ideas notebook' and before long, you will have more ideas than time to write them up.

Step 12: How to write an article

Once you have decided on the article you are planning to write – and hopefully picked out a suitable magazine or online magazine where you intend trying to place it, spend a little time thinking about how you are going to tackle writing it. You will no doubt find your own way of doing this, but if you are stuck, you could go along this route:

Begin by jotting down the information you already have, in no special order. Then do additional research via books, internet, talking to people involved or experts. However, make sure you do not get bogged down by the research.

If you have thought ahead well enough regarding what you want to say in your article, you may find yourself coming up with a list of questions that you need answers to. This can help you hone your research down to what is really necessary.

Add your own thoughts to your notes. Eventually you will end up with a higgledy piggledy mass of information. So then it is time to get it sorted into some kind of order. I imagine this as a jigsaw puzzle. All the bits are there, you just need to place them in the correct position.

The Title:

This is the first thing the editor will read, so give your article one that will catch the eye. Imagine how it will look listed in the contents section, or even boosted on the front cover. So be sure to make your title stand out in a crowd.

A title may jump out at you, or you might end up struggling for one. If it is proving difficult, consider these title 'types':

- A statement: Turn your junk into jewellery. (An article on recycling)

- A question: Who's sleeping with you tonight? (An article on bed bugs)

- A quotation: A bird in the hand. (An article on an animal sanctuary)

- A pun or play on words: Swims and Needles. (An article on hydrotherapy and acupuncture)

Hook your reader:

You need to grab your reader right from the start, so look for an opening sentence that will really catch their attention. Once hooked, do not let go. Bear in mind the magazine you are writing for, and look at their style as guidance. One little ploy is to try and use the word 'you' or 'your' in the opening paragraph as readers tend to want to know how something is going to affect them. So try and draw them in at the very start by making the article personal to them.

The body of your article

Now you slot in the 'story', that is all the information that paints the picture of what you want to say. If you have interviewed an expert, select the phrases that really have impact but be careful not to use quotes out of context. Look at sentence length and make sure your sentences are not too rambling. Short and punchy can be effective. The body of your article or feature should be full of interesting facts and information, written in a light and lively way. However, do not try and put everything into one big mass of writing. Articles can be broken up with sub headings, sidebars and fact boxes.

The end

Round your article off conclusively – maybe you can link it to the opening sentences, coming full circle. Be sure that you do not just end your article without a final summing up sentence or it will look as if you have just got exhausted. And while you may be exhausted, you do not want anyone else to know that.

Step 13: Illustrating your article

A picture paints a thousand words, and certainly it is a lot easier to sell an article if it has illustrations with it. If you can learn to take your own photographs, this will come in very useful, but of course photography – particularly to magazine quality is far from easy.

If you intend taking your own photographs, set your camera to its highest dpi. Industry standard is 300dpi. Most people would work on automatic but with some photographic education, understanding shade, depth of field and focusing can make your finished article acceptable or even excellent.

Plan ahead if you are considering writing on a subject that needs photography and decide whether it is going to be beyond your capabilities. The last thing you want is to promise an editor a feature, and then let him down on the photography.

Many people, places and topics often have their own professionally-taken 'stock' pictures, which you can gain access to, simply by asking. Companies, organisations, tourist attractions etc., generally have a Press Office who will be glad to send you jpg images if you contact them explaining your intentions. Some organisations may want to charge you for using their photographs – and only you can decide whether to take this route. You will also probably have to credit the photographer/company for the images, which means you add a note to your covering letter when submitting the pictures to a magazines editor saying something like: Would you please credit the photographs to XYZ Photography Ltd (or whoever).

Incidentally, if you are sending photographs to accompany an article, be sure to include a list of captions, e.g.:

DSC 0023: Sculptress Mary Green with her life sized cardboard model of a unicorn.

DSC 0024: Artist John Brown with his painting of an ostrich.

Step 14: Editing and polishing your article

Whatever you are writing you should never be satisfied with your first draft. Editing and polishing your writing will improve it enormously but you need to develop a critical eye regarding your own work.

Every word should count and your work should not be full of waffle and padding. Presentation should also look perfect. There is no place for spelling and punctuation mistakes. So get into the habit of making sure all your work is to the highest standard and be consistent. However, polishing your writing is much more than checking your grammar, spelling and punctuation.

Whether you are writing fiction or non-fiction, whether you are writing in the hope of getting published, or writing something such as a family history for a smaller but nonetheless equally important readership – your work still has to read as a polished, professional, captivating piece of writing which your readers will not be able to put down – whether that reader is a glossy magazine editor or your Great Aunt Joan.

The length of time you spend on revision will depend on how carefully you wrote the first draft. Some writers like to finish the whole novel/story/article before polishing. Others have to perfect each chapter/section/paragraph before moving on to the next.

So here are some things to look out for when you are polishing your work:

Look at the euphony of each sentence and paragraph – listen to the rhythm as you read it aloud to yourself. Maybe a sentence needs just an additional word putting in or taken out to make it flow more smoothly. Or maybe the punctuation needs altering slightly.

Watch out for 'purple passage'. These are over-wordy, flowery piece of writing with too many adjectives, adverbs and clichés. Look at your phrasing and consider whether you could re-phrase it to create a better harmony. Stating less rather than more allows the reader the freedom of his own imagination.

Be sure any researched information does not look as if it has been 'lifted' straight from a technical book. Make sure your work is all in your voice and your style.

Step 15: The professional approach

Whether your writing is targeted towards a top glossy magazine or it is an ode to your cat, you need to present it as perfectly as possible. And while your cat will love you whatever you do, magazine editors are not so forgiving.

So, if your writing is to stand the best possible chance of being read, accepted and published, then it needs to look professional. Editors receive many hundreds of manuscripts every week. Undoubtedly many of them are carelessly presented – much to the frustration and annoyance of the editors, who are basically looking for well written pieces of work suitable for their publication.

Maybe an editor will be willing to struggle through badly presented work in case there is a hidden gem there, but chances are they might just give it the briefest of glances and reject it purely because they have not the time or the inclination to re-work the piece even if it is fairly good.

So give your work the very best chance by making it stand out from the crowd by its professional presentation. Simply neat, legible and concise –

and of course, well written.

Many magazine editors appreciate an enquiry letter for ideas you may have for articles and features. This helps them plan ahead, and of course it is far better for you to know whether an editor is interested before you have gone ahead and written it. Here however I must admit that I do not always follow my own good advice, and on many occasions I have written an article because the subject interested me, and have then gone in search for a suitable magazine. The chicken and the egg syndrome springs to mind.

When sending a query letter or email for an article proposal, explain what your article is about in a way that will hopefully grab the editor's attention. Your writing skills start here with the query letter. If you send a dull boring or poorly thought out enquiry letter, they may get the impression that the article itself will be dull boring and poorly thought out.

It might be pertinent to say why you have written the article, particularly if you are 'qualified' in some way to write it. You could ask whether your suggested length for the article is suitable or ask if they would prefer a different word length – and be adaptable. Never write in stone. Editors like to be able to work comfortably with a writer and one who would not dream of altering one of their precious words is unlikely to get many editorial commissions. It is quite in order to ask what the payment is for freelance contributions. Alternatively offer the article/story to them 'at their usual rates'. You could offer to send the article on spec, which means you are not asking them to commission you in advance for the article, but you would be happy to write it and send it in the hope that they will like it and use it.

Just to reiterate, like any piece of writing, go over and over your enquiry letter checking for spelling mistakes, and to make sure you have put your suggestion over in a manner good enough to attract an editor. A badly written enquiry letter will indicate the same standard of article or story.

Presentation

Your work must be neatly typed, double spaced on one side of A4 white paper. Novel-length manuscripts need just a strong elastic band around them, do not bind in a ring binder, or slippery plastic folders. An article or short story can be held together simply with a paper clip.

If you are emailing your work, save it in a compatible format with the magazine's requirements, and as with hard copy, your writing should be neatly typed, double spaced (unless the magazine requests otherwise), with the pages numbered. Whether you are sending by email or hard copy be sure to also include a cover page, which gives the title of the story/article, word length, your name and contact details.

Words of Wisdom

If you are writing non-fiction, make sure you get your facts right. Much of my writing is on environmental issues and some of it is considered contentious. If you don't want to be shot down in flames, double check everything and make sure you get your work checked by a knowledgeable third-party. If you are quoting facts or statistics from elsewhere, always provide your references. If you are saying something that is contentious, tell people that this is a contentious issue and explain why. If you are giving your own viewpoint, make it clear that this is only a viewpoint. If you back up a viewpoint with statistics make sure you are using statistics to illuminate your writing and not bash people over the head with them!

Michael Boxwell

Exercise 1

Study a few magazine articles and try to work out the author's thought processes in writing a particular article in *that* way. Consider how they must have gone about it to achieve the finished product.

Exercise 2

Ask yourself: what made it so interesting to the editor who bought it? And: what made it so interesting to you – the reader? Try and apply the same thought process to your own ideas.

Exercise 3

Plan to write a 750 – 1,000 word article on a topic of your choice. Refer back to your original list of things you know about, if you need some ideas. Target your article towards a suitable magazine that you have read a number of issues of. Do whatever research is necessary.

Exercise 4

Write your article remembering to include (if relevant) quotes, sidebars, a fact box, further information website/organisation. Put the article aside for a day or two.

Exercise 5

Read your article aloud and then polish until it is word perfect. Type it up as professionally as possible, include a title page, and a brief covering letter to the editor and when you feel it is the best you can possibly do, send it off and get on with another piece of writing.

Tip

Once you start sending your work off to different markets try to keep up a constant flow of work. If you only send one thing out and then sit waiting for the postman or emailed reply it can be very disheartening. Just let it go and get on with your next writing project.

Chapter Six:
Writing Fiction

Step 16: Finding ideas

Before you can embark on a story you need at least the spark of an idea. That spark might come in the shape of a character, some real life happening, a theme, an emotion – or any number of things. The tiniest little incident, sound or thought can spark an idea for a story. The trick is to catch hold of that spark and hold onto it until you can develop it into something more substantial.

An idea for a story can occur to you at any time. It might be a chance overheard remark, it might be the sight of someone walking down the street, it might be a dream or nightmare, it could be something you read in the newspaper or see on television. Often ideas hit you when you are visiting new places – when you are on holiday or taking an excursion. For me, buildings often invoke ideas. Houses in particular, especially derelict ones!

From my own experience, I have produced successful books, stories and articles from these 'sparks'. My brother buying a canal boat that had been abandoned resulted in *Fishing for Clues*. Driving past open-curtained windows at night resulted in *Pushing his Luck*. A music concert led to *Stealing the Show* being written. It was a holiday in the Isle of Wight that prompted me to write *Disaster Bay*. A man walking down the street gave me the idea for a short story called *The Magic of Christmas*. A newspaper headline prompted me to write a vampire story. An overheard conversation between two men talking about a tank provided me with the previously mentioned article which earned me £250. A crumpled tin can, a pendant; a visit to a museum; a derelict house; a paper boy delivering newspapers; a cobweb strewn window – these have all resulted in stories or articles, and the list goes on…

File those ideas safely away

Ideas can flit in and out of your head all day long, so be sure to keep an ideas notebook and write your ideas down before they are lost to you. You could also keep a file on newspaper cuttings – news items and photographs that catch your eye which might form the basis or background to a story. Cut out and keep snippets that interest you, you never know when they might come in useful. Objects of all kinds can often inspire you to write 'around' them. Wander around a car boot sale, or an antiques shop, or an auctioneer's sales-room, or an art gallery and allow your imagination to wander.

Developing ideas

It only takes a spark of an idea to inspire you to write. But a spark is not a story, so how do you expand a spark into a fully fledged story?

Well, your idea might develop in your head, or you might find it easier to get notes written down on paper or computer. With luck your idea might unfold itself from start to finish with a logical string of events and action that simply needs writing down. On the other hand it could be a confusing jumble of images and thoughts with no clear path in sight at all.

Perhaps your idea is the ending. You visualize a scene crammed full of action or emotion, but you have no idea of the events or characters that have lead up to this point.

Basically, you have a spark of an idea which will not be ignored. So you need to expand on your idea. You need to develop a whole storyline and to do this you need to create characters.

It may be that your characters have introduced themselves to you in your head already. Perhaps a character was the initial spark, so spend time thinking about them – getting to know them because they will be taking a leading role in your story.

It could be the setting that is your spark. If so, you will need to research that area or allow it to develop in your mind or on paper. Begin writing what you already know or feel and see where this takes you. Then think about the characters who will be occupying this setting of yours.

Maybe it is an emotion that has ignited your desire to write the story. If so, you then need to develop the characters who will be experiencing that emotion. Likewise if it is an object, a headline, a snippet of conversation – whatever has sparked an idea, you then need to create characters through which the story will be told.

The spark for my 'Beast trilogy' (*The Beast, The Reawakening* and *Rampage*) came when holidaying in the Highlands of Scotland. Sunlight sparkling off the mountain tops kept catching my eye, making me think I could see something but when I looked there was nothing untoward there. That was my spark of an idea. I began developing this idea. *Maybe there is something up there, watching...*

In my head I came up with lots of 'what ifs'. What if it's a dangerous animal living in the mountains? What if it's growing angrier by the second and decides to stalk some unwitting holidaymaker? What if… and so on. Once I had decided there was definitely something up there in the mountains which was decidedly dangerous, the actual revelation of what that creature/character was came when I visited a little museum on that same holiday and saw the skull of a particular type of animal. Development of the story was under way.

If I had not held onto the initial spark of the idea, these books would never have been written.

So treasure those sparks and ideas and store them safely away.

Words of Wisdom

"Writing is hard work. George Orwell once said that writing a book is like suffering from a long bout of illness. However, no matter what the demands of the work, the sense of achievement you feel at the end of it makes any amount of suffering worthwhile! Never give up."
Simon Cheshire.

Exercise 1

Ensure that you have an ideas notebook, folder, computer file or box in which to store your ideas.

Exercise 2

Make a list of five ideas for stories. Hold back from thinking the story through yet, just save whatever 'sparks' you come up with. Maybe you will refer back to your original list – maybe not. File these ideas safely away for the moment.

Exercise 3

We will be talking about characters and plot later in this book. But for now as a good exercise, try and write the opening few paragraphs that stem from one of your ideas.

Exercise 4

Begin to think about one of the characters who might be in this story. Just for fun write a conversation between you and this character, asking him/her/it if they will take part in your story. Find out if they are up to the challenge. No doubt that character will have a few questions to ask you in return.

Exercise 5

Sticking with the same idea, write a descriptive piece about a possible setting for the story.

Tip

When you have an idea, never rely simply on memory. Write it down or it will evaporate into thin air before you know it. And when it comes to making a start in turning that idea into a story be sure that the idea excites you, because if you are not excited about it, then no one else will be either.

Chapter Seven: Characters

Step 17: Bring in your characters

The reason that people read fiction is for enjoyment and relaxation. People's working days are full with all kinds of demanding activities and responsibilities, to read is to escape that routine, if only for a short while. Therefore people need writers to create those places where they can escape to. They want intriguing story lines to follow, and they want fascinating characters to become involved with.

If you were to ask yourself why you sit down and read a book from beginning to end, you would most likely say it is because you want to find out what happens to the characters in the book. You do not think of them as being the figment of someone's imagination. To the reader these characters are real people involved in real situations.

Therefore the characters that you create need to be real rounded characters, not wooden or flat cardboard caricatures. Your characters are the most important part of your story. Without interesting characters which your readers can get to know and care about, your story will be tossed aside and left unread.

Where do characters come from?

Where do these amazing characters we read about in books, come from? Does the author use people they know in real life, or simply conjure characters up from thin air? Ask any author where their characters come from and they probably would not be able to tell you exactly. Partly it is a case of the author consciously or subconsciously drawing on their own experiences of people they have seen, heard or met. This mingled with our basic understanding of human nature and behaviour may result in a new character slowly emerging. On the other hand, perhaps your character might simply jump into your head from nowhere speaking words, acting out scenes and behaving in a way that you have no control over. If that happens, all you can do is be thankful and get their activities and adventures written down as swiftly as possible and work on them later.

Some novice writers make the mistake of basing a fictional character too closely on a real person. This is a big mistake because no matter how well you know that person, you will not know their every thought, their every action, their every hope, dream and fear. And you need to know all that and more if your characters are to appear real and are living their own lives rather than the author directing them and pulling the strings.

Caring about characters

The most important thing about your character is that you want your reader to *care*. If the reader does not care, he will not read on. So if you want readers to care, then *you* must care passionately about your characters and feel intensely involved with them. Speaking personally, I confess that I do not always know my characters well before I start writing. Sometimes it is only as I write that their true personalities begin to reveal themselves to me. I discover their moods, their fears, their humour – or lack of it, their abilities, likes and dislikes. Often a character will surprise the author by the things they say and do, and sometimes you surprise yourself by introducing something into a scene which later is vital to the story – although you had not known it at the time. On the other hand as you get well into the story you realise things are missing from the start and so you have to go back and add to the early foundations.

When it comes to creating your characters they need to be believable, not wooden or cardboard cut-outs. They need to move and have emotions, moods, be aware of what is around them, they need to use their senses. To begin with, these fictional characters only exist in the writer's head. It is only through the author's skill in using the right words that he/she will enable the reader to see, hear and believe in these characters and events. It is the writer's job to paint a vivid picture in words so the reader can see for themselves.

First impressions

As in real life, first impressions count, so aim to paint a vividly clear picture when you first introduce a character into your story. However, be careful not to write too large a chunk of description which the reader will not fully digest. Much better to reveal your character in smaller snippets of description as the story unfolds.

By having your character *doing* something, you can convey so much through their actions. As well as appearance you can reveal something of their personality and their mood by the way they go about this activity. Showing your character doing something will conjure up a picture for the reader to hang on to. By showing them moving rather than static will make them more memorable in the reader's eyes. Be aware that the way a character walks and moves says a lot about them – and remember that a character's current mood will affect their mannerisms and conduct.

Opportunities to show appearance

The opportunities to show how a character actually looks can arise through a variety of ways. For example: through a mirror; a shop window; a train window at night; a photograph of themselves etc. Although these ploys have been done many times, in the right hands these descriptions can come across brilliantly. However, try if you can to find your own original way of showing appearance.

Speaking volumes

When writing your descriptions you might want to concentrate on one aspect of your character that speaks volumes about them. A habit for example, such as fingers or feet constantly tapping; nibbling of a thumbnail; fiddling with their hair; a nervous laugh; their cheerful or off-tune singing; their whistling; their clumsiness; the sharp clip of their boots; their constant fidgeting. By giving them a 'tag' this can be linked to the character throughout the story.

Visualise your character

Before you can write anything of course, you need to see your character in your mind's eye, even if it is just a vague image. Once you start to write about him/her they will become much clearer to you. Gradually as you get to know their background, their skills, their personalities, their fears, their dreams and so on, they will start to become real. As you start to colour in your sketchy outline and fill in the blanks, your character will become a living, breathing person with a mind and attitude of their own; with a background and a life that involves others. He or she will be a person who has hopes, dreams and aspirations of their own.

While you need to know what your character looks like, it is not just appearance that makes a character. Here are some aspects to think about, you will probably think of more:

- **Appearance:** Male/female; age; marital status; height; weight; colouring; hair style; clothing; mannerisms; gait; habits; scent/smell; voice.

- **Normal life:** Address; job; education; intelligence; financial situation; hobbies and interests; family circle; friends; relationships; enemies; skills; fears and phobias; favourite things; likes and dislikes; aim in life.

- **Personality:** Shy/outgoing; talkative/quiet; moody/cheerful; thoughtful/thoughtless; kind/unkind; forgiving/unforgiving; sense of humour; calm/easily angered; opinion on political issues/religion and topical issues.

- **Background:** Past experiences shape a personality. The way others look at them and regard them adds to their persona. Plus of course, their current situation affects their moods and behaviour.

As well as knowing your characters, you also need to understand them. It is not enough to have one character disliking another – you must understand how and why that came about and know the reasons why these characters behave as they do.

Probably only a fraction of this information will come to light in your story, but if you know all this and more, your character will be real to you. Whatever they do will be true to themselves and you will have a fully fledged individual ready to leap into action.

Step 18: Naming your characters

Finding the right name for your characters is really important, and sometimes you may find that you cannot quite get going with a story until you have the names right. You will know from your own experience that different names conjure up different images so the writer's own experiences will affect their decisions on names. It is worth remembering that names can be lengthened or shortened, which I often find useful as it can show the mood of another character or reflect the atmosphere of the scene by the way one character addresses another.

Names may also indicate the age of a character along with class and the period of history in which the story is set. For example you are not likely to find a Kylie, Darren or Kevin in an historical novel. So research names of the era for authenticity. Plus of course, the background and nationality of characters will also have a bearing on their name.

Names may also reflect on whether you want your character to come across as the hero, villain or a minor character. You would hardly give the best name you have thought of to a minor character, would you? Maybe your character gets called by his surname by certain other characters. Or just the opposite – someone suddenly being called by his surname will certainly have an affect on the tone of the scene. And do not forget nicknames – but let there be a reason behind the nickname.

Avoid making your character's names sound too similar to each other. Consider going for contrast to avoid confusion. When thinking of a character's Christian name and surname, you might want to contrast them too. Perhaps if you have got a flamboyant first name, let the surname be plainer – and vice versa. But on the other hand, two plain names may sit nicely together and instantly conjure up what that character is like or looks like. Similarly, two flamboyant names together may work well. The choice is entirely yours so give plenty of thought to your characters' names before you christen them.

Step 19: Reasons why characters appear wooden

Although your characters are not real people, they must give the impression of being real people. However, if they come across as 'wooden' or are rejected by an editor as being unrealistic, here are a few suggestions as to what may have gone wrong:

- Perhaps your characters have failed to move on or develop in some way despite what they have gone through in the story. So be sure your main characters are not exactly the same at the end as they were at the beginning. They should have grown in some way.

- Possibly the author does not know his characters well enough so words and actions seem to be forced out of them, rather than the character speaking and behaving naturally. If you are forcing your characters to do and say things, get to know them better, so that they take the lead.

- Have you made your characters too good or too bad? Although you want the reader to like and care about your hero/heroine, they should not be too perfect, give them a fault or two. Likewise do not let your villain be all bad, let them have some redeeming feature.

- Too much narrated description can result in the character not revealing their personality through their own words, actions, reactions and interactions with others in the story. In other words the narrator has told the reader everything rather than allowing the character freedom to express themselves.

- Are your characters too similar? If so bring in some contrast. For example if one person is tidy make another sloppy; if one is brash make the other softly spoken; if one is a dreamer give another a practical nature. However, be sure this is done subtly and not too obvious.

Words of Wisdom

*"My best ideas happen when I play. When the pressure's off –
often when I sit down to read or enjoy the garden and do not
intend to write at all, suddenly something beeps inside my head
and I have to look for a pen and paper. Of course, a lot of what we
do as writers is disciplined, hard grind. I am a great believer in
sitting down at my desk at 9am in the morning, and in keeping to a
minimum word count per day, especially when working on later
drafts and editing, perseverance and dedication are what count.
But without time to play, the ideas dry up. So my advice to all
writers would be – make time to play."*

Rosalie Warren

Exercise 1

Working on the character you began earlier – or start something brand new, write a character sketch for them. Give yourself a time limit – about fifteen minutes. So, notepad or computer screen at the ready? Okay, think of a man, woman, child or creature. Now give them a name, age, appearance. Make a list of ten things about them. Be sure to include what they fear most.

Exercise 2

If you have not already done so, include in your character sketch what their main aim in life is at the moment.

Exercise 3

To help you to visualise this character, write a 'throw-away' scene where they are doing something quite mundane. Perhaps preparing a meal; getting dressed to go out; driving their vehicle – any 'ordinary' scenario, just so you can begin to get to know them.

Exercise 4

Now write another short scene where something is really annoying them. Perhaps they have locked themselves out of the house. Perhaps they have got a flat tyre. Maybe they cannot get their own way. Now how do they behave?

Exercise 5

Re-read exercise 2 bearing in mind their main aim in life at the moment, now put an obstacle in their path. It can be a physical or emotional obstacle (or even both). To make this obstacle more challenging, let it be connected in some way to what they fear most. Now write a short scene where your character comes face to face with this obstacle/fear.

Tip

Carry a small notebook and pen with you to note down first impressions of people you see before that impression fades away. Keep a record of these 'impressions' to call on when you are looking for ideas for characters.

Chapter Eight:
Style

Step 20: Developing your own unique style

If you take a look at the great writers of the past, names which spring to mind might be William Shakespeare, Charles Dickens, George Eliot, Jane Austen or any of the other classic writers from long ago. There is no doubt that these writers were great, their work has withstood the test of time. But as they picked up their pens – or quills in some cases, they could never have imagined that their stories would still be being read centuries on. Most probably, as they sat down to write they were feeling just as apprehensive and uncertain about getting their thoughts and ideas down on paper, as any novice or experienced writer of today.

Talk to any of today's brilliant writers – even the award winning ones and those who are household names and they are just as likely to talk about their difficulties, problems, hang ups and uncertainties in trying to craft out the sentences to enable their stories to be written. Writers from the past and present are rarely satisfied with their first and early efforts of any piece of fiction. There will always be lots of re-writing before they can be completely satisfied with their efforts – and maybe not even then.

Nevertheless, writers whose books we know and admire have persevered, and those efforts have been rewarded because their books are published, enjoyed and remembered. Stories written centuries ago are still read and enjoyed in today's modern world. At the same time, today's authors see their books on sale and read the reviews of what people have to say about their stories and their writing style.

Think for a minute about your favourite authors. If you were to analyse why you enjoy their books so much, you might say:

- They write a cracking good tale.

- The plot is always believable yet full of unexpected twists and turns.

- The characters seem like real people who you become involved with.

- Stories are full of suspense, impossible to put down.

- Their writing is beautiful – simply a joy to read.

- Their descriptions paint vivid scenes that you can really see.

- The stories are full of emotion, making you laugh and cry.

- The stories are thought provoking.

Whatever it is about the way an author has captured your interest, it is unlikely that you would say: "Well I liked this book because it reminded me of a book I read by so-and-so."

The books that you have read and enjoyed have all been written in that author's own style, their own voice. They have written it in the way that was natural to them.

Reading is important to writers. Analysing the way certain authors write their stories can be a useful lesson in creativity, but to try and imitate their style is pointless. However, the public could be waiting for *your* book, written as only *you* can – in your own unique style.

So when you think about your own style, do not fret and worry that you will never be able to write like Charles Dickens or Agatha Christie or Stephen King or J K Rowling or any other famous name – because no one is expecting you to and no one wants you to. Your style will come from you, and only you. It will be *your* unique style.

Publishers say they are looking for originality – therefore *you* have what they need. We are all unique in our own way. There is no one else quite like you. No one thinks or acts or writes like you. So if you write in your own style, being true to yourself, then that originality will shine through.

Take note though that you will not find your own style by thinking about it too much – you will find it by writing. The more you write, the more your style will develop. You may not even notice that you have a particular style, but others will. However, your style must constantly be worked at and improved upon by writing and re-writing.

If your style is to simply write the first thing that comes into your head, and leave it that way, then it will be your own style but it probably will not be anything to write home about.

Re-writing your work is as important as getting it down in the first place. If you do not work at getting the very best from your writing, then you are not being true to yourself, and success will be a long time coming.

- Your style is you along with the words you choose to use; the way you place them – your skill in arranging them to the best effect.

- Your style is the ideas for story-lines and characters that you come up with and how you deal with them.

- And your style is the way you re-work your writing. Your style is how you go about writing your story and making it work.

Improving your style

To write good fiction, it is essential to understand basic grammar and punctuation. Reading your work aloud will help you to identify any incorrect grammar so that you can rectify it.

Punctuation

Incorrect punctuation is annoying to readers and editors alike. Although a story gets copy-edited before being published, the author should ensure their writing is up to an acceptable standard in the first place. Do not expect anyone else to correct your mistakes – that is your job. Additionally, your punctuation can either make your writing flow beautifully, thereby creating the desired pace and emotion; or it can be jerky and uncomfortable, leaving the reader breathless and confused. So take care with punctuation – especially around dialogue.

Paragraphs

There are no hard and fast rules as to the length of a paragraph. Basically, just as a sentence centres around one statement, then a paragraph elaborates on that idea. When that has been dealt with then a new paragraph begins.

Variety

When writing fiction, ideally you need a variety of short paragraphs and longer paragraphs. If your page is a continuation of short paragraphs, it could become irritating to the reader. If it is one big chunk of words without a break, it could become boring.

Clichés

Your style will not benefit from the use of well-worn clichés – those stereotyped expressions that roll off the tongue (or keyboard) at the drop of a hat (sorry – two, maybe three clichés in one sentence). Find your own unique way of saying what you want to say.

Adjectives

Be careful not to use adjectives too frequently as they can have a deadening effect on a piece of work. Instead, find ways of narrating your story without littering it with adjectives, you will find the result is far more alive and colourful than you would ever have imagined.

Adverbs

While you might think adding adverbs to enhance your dialogue will improve your work, the opposite is often the truth. Use adverbs sparingly.

Words

When looking for the correct word to use, choose the most natural sounding word. Do not try to impress with some pompous word that you have had to search for in the hope of proving your superior intelligence and knowledge. The aim is not to make the reader reach for the dictionary. But on the other hand, if an obscure word is the correct word and no other word will do, then use that word with confidence.

Euphony

The euphony of each sentence has a strong bearing on your style. Read your work aloud and listen to the poetry of each sentence. If your sentences sound awkward or ugly, then re-write them, it might only be a matter of slight re-arrangement, or the addition or deletion of a word or comma, but it may make all the difference.

Words of Wisdom

"When you write, you're putting yourself on the page. Your manipulation of ideas, your choice of words, the fluidity of your text – all these things reflect your intellectual abilities. In other words, they demonstrate the quality of your thinking. Think of writing as performing two main functions: giving shape to your thoughts, and communicating those thoughts to others."
Bill Kirton.

Exercise 1

Write simply for the next three minutes, without a great deal of pre-thought, on one of these topics: your pet; your job, your hobby; your house or your garden.

Exercise 2

Read what you have just written. Save this original piece of writing to look back at but now write it again, looking to see if you can phrase sentences differently to bring in more life, colour and emotion into the piece. Having made a start, do you find there is more to say about the subject? Keep writing and see where it leads you.

Exercise 3

Now look at the punctuation and see if you have created an easy to read passage. Read it quietly to yourself, taking pauses *only* where you have put your punctuation marks – not when *you* need to take a breath. Listen to the 'poetry' (euphony) of each sentence and adjust so that each sentence flows.

Exercise 4

Write a descriptive piece of around 200 words on another of those topics without using any adjectives (describing words). When you have finished add just one adjective. Make it count!

Exercise 5

Sticking with those topics, write a short piece of dialogue (speech) between two characters who are discussing that topic.

Tip

If you are self-publishing a book, it is money well spent to get a freelance copy-editor to go through your manuscript before publishing.

Chapter Nine:
Structure

Step 21: Giving your story structure

Vital to any story is structure. Your story needs to travel from beginning to end with increasing conflict, tension and interest along the way. Your story also needs characters. So to begin with expand on what you have.

Characters

If characters have inspired you to write, then flesh those characters out. Get to know them. Know their aims and ambitions, and be clear what problems or obstacles are stopping them from achieving their goals.

Setting

The setting for your story may be the spark that has inspired you to write. So whether it is a jungle in a war torn country or a quaint English tea shop, your next step is to introduce characters into that setting. Begin with by asking yourself what sort of person would – or would not be there?

Theme

Maybe it is a theme that has struck a chord with you such as *Love conquerors all* or *Revenge is sweet*. Or perhaps it is 'a moment in time' – such as a snapshot that strikes you as so poignant you need to write a story around it. Develop what you have so far; expand on what you see in your thoughts, bring characters to life and create the backdrop in which your drama can unfold.

Conflict

Your story needs conflict. There must be some sort of difficulty or obstacle marring your character's progress or their aim in achieving their goal. Even the most gentle of stories needs conflict. Conflict does not (necessarily) mean bombs dropping, guns blazing and people at loggerheads with one another. Conflict comes in all shapes and sizes, for example a character's inner turmoil of making the correct decision, or battling against their own conscience. Conflict can be physical or emotional, or a mixture of both. Be sure that your story has conflict of some sort.

Step 22: Viewpoint

Some writers, to begin with are not sure what is meant by viewpoint. Viewpoint is through whose eyes and heart the story is told. So write your story through the eyes and heart and viewpoint of your main character – the person with some obstacle to overcome or dilemma to sort out. It is important that the conflict in the story affects this main character personally, so that we experience all their anxieties, sorrow and joy. If the reader fails to connect with this person they probably will not read on. There are a variety of viewpoint to choose from – some of which you should avoid at all costs.

Third Person Viewpoint

In my opinion, the most workable viewpoint to choose. Here, the character is referred to by name, or by he or she. The reader becomes involved in the story through this viewpoint character and will be able to identify with them.

First Person Viewpoint

This is another popular choice, with 'I' being the main character. Possibly novice writers feel that they cannot go wrong, if 'I' is the key character. But beware not to simply 'tell' the reader what is going on, rather than fully dramatizing each scene. This could result with an effect that 'I' is just standing on the sidelines, reporting on the story without ever really getting involved. Remember too, that 'I' (unless this is your autobiography) is still a character. It is not you, the author. It is a character with all the traits and characteristics of any fictional character. So 'I' must stay in character. Do not think you can do away with the work of creating a fully rounded believable character because you are 'it'. There are no short-cuts to be gained by writing in the first person.

Single Viewpoint

Written through the viewpoint of just the main character. The reader will see, hear, think and feel what this character does but they will not know the innermost thoughts and emotions of anyone else.

Multi Viewpoints

Here you choose another character – or characters through whose eyes, ears and emotions we view certain scenes/chapters. Seeing things through another character's eyes can be vital to your story, so choose your viewpoint characters carefully and plan when you will be switching viewpoint. Make sure it is at the start of a new chapter, or a major scene break. Be sure that you are not jumping from one character's head to another every few moments.

Skipping viewpoint

To write a story where everybody's viewpoint is given is, in my opinion, a bad idea. If you are constantly skipping from one character to another the reader will not be able to identify with any of the characters and undoubtedly lose interest in the whole thing.

Omniscient Viewpoint

Another one to be avoided. This is the godlike approach knowing all things and everyone's thoughts. Unless you are a very skilled writer, stories written in this way give the feeling that you are just looking in – observing what is going on, rather then being involved with your characters. If you decide on using everybody's viewpoint, beware that it is the perfect way of making your story nobody's.

Step 23: Choosing which tense to write in

Whether you are writing in the third person viewpoint, the first person viewpoint, or multi viewpoints, you need to decide which tense works best for you and this particular story.

Past Tense

This is the most serviceable and manageable tense to write in. Here the character acted in a certain manner, your characters 'said' and 'thought' which although are in the past there is still that immediacy to it all.

Present Tense

This is not an easy tense to write it, particularly to master it and stick with throughout a novel. Some experienced authors are expert at it, but get it slightly wrong and it jars the reader and makes for an uncomfortable read. However, if skilfully done, you can switch from present tense to scenes/chapters written in the past tense when your character is thinking back on events.

Step 24: Plotting and Planning

Plotting – planning, call it what you will. Stories do not appear by magic, they have to be worked at and crafted. You cannot possibly know every twist and turn your story will take, but even a vague outline of storyline will assist you to make sense of what you are working on. Breaking your story down into manageable chunks is a way of being kind to yourself with regard to your writing.

Storyline

Try and draft out your storyline. Beginning, middle and an end is a start – one, two, three. Or you could make a list of say, 1 – 30 or even 1 – 10 or 1 – 100. It depends on how clearly you see your story at this early stage.

The Beginning

Think about your opening scene. Jot down points that need to be written in early on, for example, the introduction of certain characters; the establishing of the conflict and mood; the setting. Number these points if you wish. You will probably find yourself re-arranging the order of things happening – which is good because your planning will be starting to take shape.

The Middle

At this stage you certainly will not have all the events and action sorted in your head. These will come gradually as a result of your characters' interactions with each other and the situations they are in. However, there may be key incidents that you know should occur so jot these down as bullet points in your skeleton. You may also want to introduce other threads (sub plots) into your story. You might want to make the problems for your main character worsen. Incidents will undoubtedly occur to you as your characters develop. Jot these points down so that you can see the shape of your story and make sure characters' problems are not resolved too early and the pace of the story is progressing nicely.

The End

You may or may not know how your story will end, but you can remind yourself here to tie up all loose ends of your story lines and sub plots. Be sure that this is where the climax of the story comes – the point where your character wins or loses, achieves his goal or fails. Your final bullet point in your structure may be your key character's last words or thoughts or emotions on the outcome.

Structuring your story

Your story structure may be vague or highly detailed, or somewhere in between. Think of it as a guideline which you can follow or veer away from as you write. It is simply there as a rough guide for when you need it. However there is no hard and fast way of working on your story's structure. Some writers may not even realise they are structuring their story, allowing it to unfold at will. This is fine if it works for you, but the last thing you want to do is write yourself into a corner – a dead end with nowhere to turn. So developing your plot and story structure is a sound way of proceeding.

Some writers may think that plotting and structuring in this manner will hinder their creative streak or stop the characters from developing. Just remember that your structure is not carved in stone, you can change things at any time. It is merely a guide so you do not get lost. And best of all, when you can see your story in 'bullet points' that seemingly overwhelming task of writing a story from beginning to end is not as daunting as it was when you were just faced with a spark of an idea.

Scene by scene

Personally, I tend to think in scenes rather than chapters or paragraphs or sentences. I try to picture each scene of the story seeing it from the outside but then also through the eyes and emotions of my key character. I try to visualise the setting and get a feel for the atmosphere. I try and imagine the characters and see what they are doing and listen to what they are saying to each other. As I write each scene, I visualise it being acted out in my head, so that I am not floundering for the right word from a dictionary or thesaurus, I am simply writing what is happening – through the eyes of my key character.

Bring those scenes to life

Know what you want to achieve in each scene. Think of every scene as a little story in itself, yet one that leads onto the next piece of the story – the next scene. Take each scene slowly, bringing life and colour and emotion to it. Know what that scene is there for. Know what you want it to achieve in each scene and strive to attain this.

Step 25: How and when to start your story

I always find it best to start the story where there is a change to routine, something different is happening, something unusual, out of the norm – and it is causing a problem for your key character (conflict). You can start with a dramatic line of dialogue or a vivid description or an exciting piece of narrative. So long as it interests the reader and makes them want to read on, then you have achieved your aim. If your beginning is flat and dull do not relax thinking that it will be okay because it really livens up by page ten because your reader may never get that far.

The opening scene

Your opening scene is an extremely important scene. It is where you will interest a reader or editor, or lose them forever.

Ideally your first scene should:

- Hook your reader. Be sure your opening sentences are as alluring as possible. You do not have to explain everything at once or establish the logic behind the words – that can be drip fed later.

- Introduce your main character.

- Establish the conflict facing your main character.

Moving forward

As you think in scenes remember that each scene needs to carry your story forwards, with your character's problems growing more difficult all the time. One difficulty or dilemma should lead to another on the journey towards the climax and ultimate conclusion to your story. Basically, give your character a hard time and do not let them get out of trouble too easily.

Pace

Make it a roller coaster of a ride. Imagine if you were on a fairground ride and it started at the highest, fastest most terrifying moment. The rest of the ride would surely be something of an anti climax. Likewise with your story, give it a dramatic start by all means, but it should by no means be the most dramatic moment of the whole story. Be aware too, that while a story needs drama, action and emotional high spots it does not want to be high drama throughout. Give your story a mix of quieter, slower, more relaxed scenes – although never boring and always moving forward and rising gradually to a crescendo.

Hold the reader's attention

Keep them interested not only by the events happening to your characters – and your characters' reaction to events, but in the way you write these incidents. Look to the opposite ends of the scale. For example, high drama incidents hit harder if the scene before is of a slower more relaxed nature. If you are revealing betrayal it will be more acute if the reader has witnessed a previous scene of total trust. If there is a scene of joy it will be more joyful if the reader has coped with the character's sorrow beforehand. If your character is about to step into danger, then the lead up could lull the reader into thinking they were safe.

Vary your sentences

Vary their structure, length and even the choice of words, so that it might be read with a feeling of calm, or a feeling of rising tension. Longer words and sentences and descriptive passages will give a more leisurely relaxed sense of being. Short, sharp words and sentences will give the opposite effect. If you can pace your story and mix in unexpected twists and turns, then like a roller coaster ride, your readers will cling on breathlessly to the very end.

Major scenes

Stories are a mix of narrative, action and dialogue. Obviously some parts of the story can be related by narrative – this carries the story forward. However make sure that you do not narrate really important scenes. When it comes to major scenes, be sure to let your characters act them out in all their glory. Let readers experience all the emotion and drama, let them hear the actual words being spoken, and not have the scene simply skipped over by a few narrated sentences or they will feel cheated.

You will want your climax of the story to be the most dramatic of scenes, so do not risk diluting the main action by tying up the loose ends at that point. As you approach the climax, be sure that all those loose ends are nicely tied up before the climax, so that there is just one final element to be dealt with at the end, which is basically whether your main character succeeds or fails.

The climax of your story should be the blackest of black moments where you show the most intense struggle your character has yet had to face. This is the point where you really want your readers to be rooting for him/her.

Take your time over this final scene:

- Do not get lazy and brush over this vital scene with a few lines of narrative.

- Do not 'cheat' your reader by some surprise twist that is not in the least believable such as a mistake or misunderstanding that could have been sorted out at any time.

- Do not cheat your reader by the introduction of some character or random incident/coincidence that has not been part of your story throughout.

- And please do not let your character suddenly realise it had all been a dream.

Your ending should:

- See your key character succeeding in overcoming the obstacles that lay in his path.

- Your key character should have evolved and moved forward. Ideally changed for the better not the worse.

- If it is not a totally happy ending, at least give your reader hope or satisfaction that things will be better from now on.

- Leave the reader with a sense of completeness and not left with unanswered questions.

Step 26: Be self critical

Of course afterwards you will edit your work, hone and polish it. You will work on each sentence so that the euphony is just right. You will check for spelling mistakes and weed out unnecessary adjectives and adverbs, and you will read it aloud to see if the written word has conveyed what you envisaged.

Ask yourself if you have really painted a picture? Are your characters engaging – will readers care about them? Is the plot believable? How is the ending, will it leave the reader satisfied or will they be left asking questions – or worse with a feeling of being cheated?

Words of Wisdom

"Go to your local library, find the shelves covering your genre/type and pick five books at random. For each one, read the opening few pages and write down three things that make you want to read on."

Andy Seed.

Exercise 1

Working from one of the earlier exercises or a brand new idea, make a bullet point list or a numbered list of 1-30. Now fill in some of the events, action or scenes that you want to see happening in the story.

Exercise 2

From what you have, look at the high and low spots. Aim to make the high spots gradually rise as the story progresses so that each dramatic scene is more intense than the one before. You are aiming towards the climax or 'black spot' at the end of the story.

Exercise 3

Think about the mood or emotion that you want to achieve in the more dramatic scenes. Make the scene before or after contrasting in some way.

Exercise 4

Try to 'flesh out' the story structure so that you have quite a detailed synopsis to work with.

Exercise 5

Take a careful look at what you have created so far. Be honest and ask yourself whether your key character is facing some sort of conflict. Does the situation get worse before it gets better? Is the pace of your story steadily 'hotting up' or is it sinking or jumbled? Work on it until you have crafted a strong storyline.

Tip

Never sit down to a blank sheet of paper. Know what your first words are going to be. Rehearse them in your head beforehand. When you finally sit down to write them, you are already well under way.

Chapter Ten:
Dialogue

Step 27: Writing realistic dialogue

Many people struggle with writing dialogue, for others it is the easy part. The dialogue that you write has to sound realistic, not wooden nor contrived nor unnatural. In fact the words that your characters say are not like real speech at all. You only have to listen to two people talking and you will hear all the repetitions, the interruptions, the irrelevant bits, the clichés, the *umms* and *aaahs* and phrases that are just padding.

Basically, dialogue needs to give the impression of real speech but with the boring bits taken out, leaving just the words that are there for a reason.

A few lines of good dialogue can reveal more about character and plot than many pages of prose. Dialogue brings vitality to a story – it brings your story to life.

Reasons for dialogue

Dialogue is there for several reasons:

- To carry the story forward

- To characterise the speaker and other characters.

- To show the emotional state of the speaker.

- To describe or set the scene or mood.

- To increase the tension and suspense.

- To provide the reader with necessary information.

Do not mislead the reader:

Dialogue is not there to pad out your story. If something is mentioned in dialogue then it is there for a reason. The reader may not know that reason at that moment, but later in the story it should become clear. If your dialogue is littered with irrelevant, unnecessary facts that come to nothing it will slow your story down and spoil it. So keep it alive and moving forward. Do not allow your characters to get bogged down in a lot of unnecessary banter that does nothing to move the story forward.

Show don't tell through dialogue

Dialogue is the best way to reveal character, so be sure that in your story you do not simply state that your character is, for example, a bad tempered grouch; or that he was a man with a wry sarcastic wit; or that one character made another one angry by what he said. Let the reader actually *hear* the character saying the words that have labelled him a bad tempered grouch. Let them *hear* that wry sarcastic wit it action. And they want to *hear* the heated conversation between those two characters which resulted in someone getting angry.

Attributions

Attributions is the term used to describe who is speaking – *he said, she replied, I answered etc.* Some writers feel they need to look for other ways of saying who is speaking and search the thesaurus to find alternative ways of saying 'he said'. In fact the humble 'he said' is virtually invisible in the context of the story, especially when the dialogue itself is sparkling. By using an alternative it can become conspicuous – it draws importance to itself. And if your story is littered with these alternatives it can make your work look amateurish.

You can vary your character's speeches with equally unobtrusive attributions such as 'he replied' or 'he answered' or 'he asked'; and occasional 'he shouted' or 'he laughed'. However, do not feel that you need to avoid using 'said' by putting in contrived attributions such as he articulated, he beseeched, he empathized, he interjected etc. Action before dialogue can do away completely with the need for an attribution.

Dialogue is one of the best ways to show the personality of a character and the reader should know who is speaking simply by what is being said and the way it is being spoken. However, be careful not to have a whole string of one-liners without narrative or character interaction. The reader does not want to have to count back to see who is talking, so be sure you put enough information in to make it clear who is speaking.

Dialect and slang

It is often quite difficult to write dialogue for characters who come from a region or country with a strong dialect. Writers can easily get into a quandary as they try to mimic a broad accent, dropping g's and h's and struggling to write words so that the reader has to mentally form the sound in their heads as they read. Difficult to do, annoying and it looks awkward on the page. Far better to research and listen to the speech patterns and idioms from the region or slip in a word or two that indicates the locality.

Slang

Certain characters in your stories will undoubtedly need to resort to slang if they are to sound realistic but be careful not to use the latest modern day slang, which comes and goes every year or so. While it might be the way teenagers are expressing themselves today, by the time your book or story comes out, it could be very outdated and make your writing also seem 'dated'. So when using slang, stick to the good old fashioned slang words and expressions that have been around for years.

Four lettered words

For your characters to come across as real people there will be times when you have no alternative but to use a 'four letter' word. It is the only thing your character could say. A swear word may be what is needed to create the impact and show the character's mood at that time. However if you have a character who 'swears like a trooper' then lines of continual swear words will become irritating – even to the point of turning some readers away. Plus they soon lose their impact. It is worth remembering that a four letter word in a novel can be startling and effective, while a hundred will become boring.

Dialogue to start your story

A line of dialogue is the perfect tool for starting off your story. Straight away you can hook your reader and draw them in. Through dialogue you can instantly indicate the conflict and what is at stake. It can help your reader to take an instant like or dislike to a character and set the scene for what is to come.

Dialogue to end your story

Dialogue is also a perfect choice for ending your story. After all, the reader has stuck with your characters throughout your story, surely it is only fair that one of them should have the final word?

Be professional with your dialogue

Getting the punctuation around dialogue must become second nature to you. So many novice writers get the layout for fiction and dialogue wrong. Speech set within quotation marks should finish with the final punctuation mark also inside the closing quotation mark – not outside. And indent unless told by the magazine editor not to.

"It was a nightmare," Gary wailed, throwing his school bag under his desk and slumping down into his chair. "That bloke cared more about his rotten car than hitting my dog!"

Laura pulled off her gloves and woolly hat. "Poor Kess. People can be so cruel."

"I can still see his big, ugly face," Gary said, his brown eyes glittering angrily. "Said it was my fault for not having her on a lead. But Kess never needs a lead."

It is so easy to make mistakes. All those commas, full stops, quotation marks, exclamation marks, capital letters and uncapped letters – which all matter a great deal. So make sure you have it perfected. Do not expect anyone else to put it right for you, it is no one's responsibility but your own. If you have not mastered the presentation of dialogue it could spoil your chances with an editor. So get it right then enjoy your dialogue. Enjoy hearing what your characters have to say, and let their dialogue carry your story forward.

Having problems with dialogue

If your dialogue just does not sound realistic it may be because you have not created your characters well enough yet. So spend more time on getting to know them. If you are struggling to find something for them to say, then again it might be because they are not real enough to you yet or the scene has not been set dramatically enough to draw a response and a reaction from them. More ground work could be needed. Read your dialogue aloud and adjust until it sounds real.

Words of Wisdom

"Dialogue tags do so much more than tell you who's speaking. Like rests in a music score they are the heartbeat of a conversation's pace and the ebb and flow of its tension. Letting us know who said what is fine. But whether you put it at the start, at the end, or breaking up any part of a piece of speech, or even not at all can create a whole palette of shading for your dialogue."
Dan Holloway

Exercise 1

Select a point in your story and write a dozen or so lines of dialogue between two of the characters. Remember the reasons for dialogue as mentioned above. Do not let it just be padding, make it meaningful.

Exercise 2

As dialogue practice write a page or so which is mainly dialogue around this scenario: The bridegroom and best man await the arrival of the bride. The bridegroom is getting cold feet.

Exercise 3

More dialogue practice. Through dialogue let 14-year old Jack explain to his teacher why he has not brought in his homework.

Exercise 4

And yet more dialogue practice. Re-write any one of the above scenes using no other attribution except 'he/she (or name) said'. You may also use action and then speech, with no 'he saids' at all.

Exercise 5

Go through all these exercises and check your punctuation and capital/small letters are correct around your speech. If you are still not sure about this, consult a selection of dialogue from a *trusted* published book.

Tip

If you have difficulty writing dialogue, read radio plays and try your hand at writing one. Plays depend completely upon the spoken word to unfold the plot, reveal character, create suspense and finally bring the story to a climax and conclusion.

Chapter Eleven:
Narrative

Step 28: Writing the narrative

The narrative is the voice through which you tell your story. Narrative is what leads the reader smoothly through the story with all its ups and downs, high and low spots, emotions and drama. The narrative is what tells the reader what is going on. It lets the reader know that a Highland warrior is marching down the valley, kilt swinging, his beret tilted to one side. The narrative is what tells the reader that thunderous black clouds are rolling in over the rooftops and that the wind is whipping the leaves into a frenzy.

Your story is a balance of narrative and dialogue. However there is no set formula to see if you are getting the balance right, this all comes down to your ability to write a story – and that comes with practice.

You might start with narrative, setting the scene and drawing the reader into this new world. Or you might start with dialogue and then narrate the next few paragraphs to define who and where your characters are and what is going on. Narrative, like dialogue advances your story – it moves your story on.

Narration works hand in hand with viewpoint, so that the writer can merge a descriptive passage smoothly into the key character's thoughts and actions.

The setting for your story is obviously very important. And the settings will change from scene to scene. The narrative voice will portray these settings, letting the reader in on this world, which so far is a product of your imagination. Your narration as you tell the story must engage and interest the reader. It must describe scenes and characters and stir the emotions of the reader.

Through narrative you set the scene, you describe what is going on, you move the story forward. You show the reader what you can see in your mind. You have to paint the picture and open up this imaginary world where these imaginary people are battling with the many obstacles littering their path.

But be careful not to sit back in your typist's chair as you, the author describe this imaginary scene through *your* eyes. Stick closely to your viewpoint character, and let the narrative go hand in hand with their emotions.

Your own style of writing narrative will reveal itself the more you write. It is down to you to polish that style until you create scenes which are vivid, yet not too flowery. Too much and you will be writing 'purple passages' which are gushing with sentiment. Too little and your story could be dull.

There is a very fine line however in the narration of the story and the author talking – giving the reader that extra bit of information that suddenly jars them from the world of make believe and allows them to hear the author's voice. You as author, should stay well hidden – have faith and trust in your characters. If the author goes beyond the narration and pops in their own thoughts, opinions, or additional information, it instantly jolts the reader from this fictional world and reminds them that the author is still there, pulling the strings. The reader does not want that. This story is between them and the characters, the author must remain out of sight.

So find your narrative voice and let that voice speak throughout the story, linking the passages of dialogue, keeping the whole thing flowing smoothly. If you are tempted to add in some piece of random information for good measure, or to start preaching or stating an opinion, then hit the delete key, and find some natural way for your characters to pass this information on, either through their actions, their thoughts or through their dialogue.

Step 29: Handling transitions

Your characters and your readers often have to move from one place to another; from one time to another; or from one emotion to another. The device for moving smoothly from scene to scene is called a transition.

A transition might only be a few words, or it could be a number of sentences. You might need a transition to bridge a highly dramatic scene when the character needs time to think before moving on to a scene with a totally different atmosphere.

Your one or two sentences can move your story on an hour, a week, a year; or from the highlands of Scotland to a beach in the Bahamas.

In time transitions, you could use simple phrases, such as:

- The following morning…

- That evening…

- A week later…

- At the end of the week…

Here are a few transitions where there is a change of scene:

- Some miles away…

- In the train on the way back…

- Thick snow had fallen overnight…

- The drive to the hospital was agonising...

A transition should be simple and swift with the objective of getting from *here* to *there* quickly and smoothly, so that you can get on with the story.

Step 30: Flashbacks

If it is necessary to show something that happened in the character's past, which motivates and affects the characters actions, emotions and attitude towards something now, this is called a flashback.

To handle this so that it does not confuse the reader, or bring the present action to a grinding halt, the author needs to write it with care. It does not have to come in one big scene, it can be effective to weave fragments of flashbacks into the action and dialogue of your story, so the reader glimpses bits of a tantalising past.

If your flashback needs to be a complete scene or a number of scenes, then find a way of framing this section between the present action, both before and afterwards, so there is no doubt in the reader's mind when they are leaving the present to go into the past, and when they are leaving the past to return to the present.

For example it could be through a journey, with your character watching through a train window and remembering. When the flashback scenes have finished, bring the action back into the train carriage, with something immediate happening, even if it is just the ticket inspector asking for her ticket.

It could be in the middle of a conversation when the past catches up. After writing the flashback, return to the conversation with perhaps just a hint that your character has not been paying attention.

Your flashback, particularly if it is a short scene, could be revealed through dialogue. Simply have two characters talking and one telling the other about a past event.

If the event is lengthy and involves characters from the past in conversation, be very wary that the whole thing does not get confused.

And if you find you are writing most of your story as a flashback, then possibly you have started your story in the wrong place at the wrong time. A re-think might be necessary. In short stories however, this can work effectively, especially if you are looking for a twist in the tail ending. As when you return to the present towards the end of your story, you can reveal something surprising (but believable).

Step 31: Cliff-hangers

You want your readers to be gripped by your story, you want them to be unable to put your book down. You want them to keep turning the pages until the very end. And one way of ensuring they do just that is to make sure you end your chapters or scenes on a note where something is about to happen – a cliff-hanger.

While your chapter should encompass a complete section, period or scene of your story, end your chapter at a point where something is about to happen – and your reader is desperate to know what.

For children's stories in particular you can really pull out all the stops. For adult stories you need to be a little more subtle, perhaps it is no more than a hint – but none the less keep your reader hooked wondering what is going to happen next.

Whether you choose to put the readers out of their misery and continue with the present action in the next chapter/scene that is up to you. You could switch to a different thread of your story leaving the reader on tenterhooks to know what has become of the character in peril or dilemma – another ploy in keeping your reader hooked into your story.

Words of Wisdom

"There's an old Quaker saying, 'Think it possible that you may be mistaken.' It's good advice for life and also for editing! Don't be so wedded to your words that you refuse to see how they could be better. It's hard – crumbs, is it hard! – but you owe it to your story."

Joan Lennon.

Exercise 1

Write a list of around ten example transitions moving a scene from one *place* to another. e.g. *A mile further down the road...*

Exercise 2

Write a list of around ten examples transitions to indicate that a period of time has passed, e.g. *The following spring...*

Exercise 3

From exercise 2 in Chapter 10 where the scenario is a conversation between the reluctant bridegroom and best man as they wait for the bride to turn up, write the scene fully with narrative and dialogue with the groom being the key character. Reveal his innermost thoughts and emotions as well as what he is saying and doing. End the scene on a cliff-hanger. Then start another scene with a *transition* showing we are now in the viewpoint of the bride who is on her way to the church (or not). End that scene with a cliff-hanger.

Exercise 4

If you've written exercise 3 in the past tense – i.e. the characters *'said'*, *'thought'*, walked, acted, looked etc. Example: *Sarah walked into the church, faces turned to stare. No one was smiling and her heart plummeted. "Oh God!" she murmured.*

Now re-write the scene in the present tense – i.e. your characters will now *'say'*, *'think'*, walk, act, look etc. Example: *Sarah walks into the church, faces turn to stare. No one is smiling and her heart plummets. "Oh God!" she murmurs.*

Exercise 5

Choosing the tense and viewpoint you prefer from the above exercises, add in a little flashback – maybe it will be the proposal. Let it be clear where the flashback starts and ends, incorporating it with care into your scene. Treat the above as useful exercises or you may have just successfully written a nice little short story!

Tip

The setting for each scene that you write should be considered with care. Be sure you have chosen the most interesting and telling location for every scene.

Chapter Twelve:
Atmosphere and Mood

Step 32: Developing emotion, atmosphere and tension

So you have planned your story carefully, you know your characters so well they are practically your best friends, and it is all jogging along nicely. The thing is you do not want your story to jog nicely along, you want it to bring tears to your readers' eyes, or make them laugh out loud, or make them so involved they miss their bus stop or read long into the night even though they know they will struggle to get up in the morning.

Let us take a look at some of the tried and tested ways of building up the emotional atmosphere, the mood and the suspense. Of course to begin with you must have characters that appear to be real people. You must have created them so realistically that you would swear you could recognize them if they were walking down the street. Added to this, these characters – at least your key character – your hero or heroine, must be faced with a problem, dilemma or conflict that really matters. It is not a trivial matter, this is something that is deeply troubling him or her, and because the reader has identified with this person, they need to be just as troubled.

Let your characters talk to each other

Characters need to communicate with each other. Tension, conflict, anger, hatred, love, can all develop through characters talking to one another. Characters can reveal they are afraid or anxious or show the drama rising through their speech. Staccato dialogue shows their breathlessness. They do not have time to speak at length, even the narration should come across in that same short sharp manner. Dialogue that is interrupted, or the speaker stops abruptly fearing they have said too much can all help to increase the tension; the occasional… (dot dot dot) can work wonders, if used sparingly.

Location, location

Be imaginative when setting the scene. While the setting for a ghost story might well be in a graveyard in the middle of the night, it could be even more frightening if the ghost haunted an office when most of the staff had gone home; or in the sports hall of a school and only one person can see it. Why not make your location in acute contrast to the emotional theme, for example love blossoming amidst the hostilities of a war or riot; or murder at a joyful family celebration. So, try not to go for the obvious, look for contrasts to the 'norm' for the settings for your stories and individual scenes.

Changeable weather

We all complain about the weather, but writers can actually do something about it – and should. The weather can enhance a scene and add massively to the mood and atmosphere. Take note of how so many writers engage the might of Mother Nature to make a scene more dramatic. Hurricanes, storms, thunder and lightning, dense fog, a blinding blizzard…

The next time you encounter some intense weather, take careful note – make notes. Look at how the clouds roll in; see if you can taste and smell the fog, try and describe in words that smell and taste – be aware of how it disorientates you; see the different shades of sky and clouds during a thunder storm. Look at the colours of sunsets and daybreaks. Try and find the words that will describe these scenes and do them justice. Whenever you personally are drenched in a cloudburst, or freezing in a snowstorm, write up those emotions and sensations as soon as you can – no doubt they will come in useful.

Show don't tell

You will have heard that phrase many times, so be sure you are acting upon it. Your story needs to engage the emotions so it is no use simply saying that a character was feeling this way or that way; it is no good saying they were feeling angry or feeling sad. It is through the character's actions, reactions, words and thoughts that you need to *show* them being angry or being sad – or any one of the many emotions people feel, i.e.: misery, jealousy, grief, joy, empathy, sympathy, love, hate.

You could say Joe was furious. Or you could say:

To begin with Joe fell silent, and then a deepening redness coloured his cheeks and a vein began to pulsate at his temple. His eyes glittered, as if a mist had formed over them. His hands clenched into fists, his knuckles turning a shining white.

You could say Jill was jealous. Or you could say:

Jill tried to smile, tried to congratulate Claire on her engagement to Steve, but the words stuck in her throat. Her lips formed the usual shape for a smile, but even Claire looked oddly at her and Jill wondered if her smile had actually looked more like a snarl.

Use all your senses

To bring a scene to life and allow the reader to experience the events in all their glory, write using all your senses – taste, touch, smell, sound, sight – and not forgetting your sixth sense, that ability to just 'know' something.

Sight

Readers know what everyday objects look like, so pick out the unusual aspect or angle, or focus on something that has specific meaning to the character – perhaps something that brings back memories or affects their emotions in some way. To increase suspense, why not have normal everyday things suddenly appearing wrong. Remember the neatly stacked tins and folded towels in *'Sleeping with the Enemy'*? Little things associated with an unpleasant character can increase tension. Perhaps your villain smoked cigarettes, so the stub of one left on the heroine's doorstep might heighten her fear. The sight of a footprint or a large paw print in the soft earth might add tension; or the sight of something just disappearing out of sight; or the glimpse of a shadow; or the glare of car headlights hurtling towards you. Whatever you choose to mention in your narrative, let it be there for a reason.

Sound

Bring a scene to life by allowing your reader to hear the sounds that your character can hear. Think of the background noises whether your characters are in a factory, a supermarket, on a beach, in an aircraft or wherever. If there is a sound that is out of place in that situation, be sure to let the reader hear that. Let us hear the tone of someone's voice when they speak and the way that is modulated depending who they are talking to. When increasing tension, emotion and atmosphere, draw attention to sounds that may not have been noticed before. A quiet room can become even quieter if you can hear the ticking of a clock, or the soft popping of a gas fire, or the sound of their own breathing. You can heighten the suspense in a story by writing in the softest sounds – a whisper, a creak. The softest sounds are often the most affective.

Smell

We have all experienced how certain smells conjure up different memories and feelings. A certain smell can whisk you back decades. Freshly baked bread, a particular perfume or aftershave, a fish and chip shop, a sea breeze, an oily garage, bacon and eggs cooking, lilies, roses, newly mown grass, freshly ground coffee. Use your sense of smell in your writing to bring a scene to life. And when you want to emphasise the mood even more strongly, focus your character's attention on the smell of something specific and meaningful.

Taste

Your characters may taste lots of good and bad things throughout your story, but again use the ploy cleverly when you really want to arouse the emotions. Let them taste things other than food. How about the taste of their lover's lips against theirs? Or taste rain on their tongue; or snowflakes or fog. At the other end of the scale, let them taste fear – let it be so tangible that they can taste it. Perhaps they are so sickened that they taste the bile burning in their throats. What if they are so wracked with misery that their favourite food tastes like wood shavings and sticks in their throat? As people know what certain things taste like, be selective in what you choose to write about – pick out the more unusual things to taste, or when things taste wrong for some reason.

Touch

This sense can portray so much. People in love want to touch each other constantly, to be close, holding hands, caressing, cuddling. Parents hug their children; people stroke their pets; strangers do not touch and if they do, there is embarrassment and apologies for invading the other person's space. Acquaintances might shake hands. We touch and feel so many things, the silky fabric of a ball gown; the smooth surface of an expensive piece of furniture or ornament; we might touch a leather coat to feel its softness and suppleness. Let your reader feel your character's world through the sensation of touch.

6th Sense

Don't forget that sixth sense. It is very useful when you want to increase the suspense by having your character just sense something wrong. They stop in their tracks... *they just know...*

So be sensible and use all your senses.

Step 33: Step up the pace

Careful pacing of your story can add to the drama. When you have got a scene coming up which is shocking or very dramatic then the previous scene should be in contrast. Lull the reader into a false sense of security, so when the axe falls, they will not be ready for it. Hopefully they will enjoy the surprise you have given them.

Just like on a roller coaster, people want to be frightened and excited, so in fiction readers want all the ups and downs of a gripping roller coaster of a story, but unlike the track of a roller coaster, they do not want to know when the next twist is coming.

Never let your story go stale, keep throwing up unexpected twists and new developments. Do not allow your story to be predictable. Sometimes new developments may even surprise you. Avoid giving too many clues away too fast. Drip feed information to your readers.

More on cliff-hangers

As mentioned earlier, one sure way of increasing the tension and the dramatic high spot is by having cliff-hangers. Plan your scenes so that the most dramatic spot can come at a point where you can break off for a new chapter. Build each scene up to its most exciting point – then stop. A new chapter may provide fresh momentum, or you may keep your reader hanging on in suspense while you deal with another thread of your story. Maybe that too can be brought to boiling point. You could be like a circus plate spinners and have all your plates spinning precariously, balancing them just perfectly and in total control.

So go through your story and see if by re-phrasing certain sections you can add to the atmosphere or build tension. See if you can create little ploys of your own – barely noticeable things which only register in the reader's subconscious. Occasional words in italics for example; or the repetition of a word or sentence that turns it into something poignant or sinister. Could you subtly hint that disaster is soon to befall the character? Could there be a recurring thought, word or phrase that jabs at your character when things are getting tricky? Experiment with your writing and see what works and what doesn't.

Words of Wisdom

"Remember why you are writing – it's not to impress but to express. There's a huge difference between spoken and written language. When we speak, we use gestures, tone of voice, pauses and all sorts of other tricks to convey exactly what we mean. It's easy to signal to someone that you're being sarcastic, playful or serious, or when you want to emphasise a word or a point. When we write things, however, it's not that easy. That's why we need to make the most of the feature that does help readers to interpret our intentions more easily – punctuation. It helps us to separate or link ideas, to stress some and give relatively less importance to others."

Bill Kirton.

Exercise 1

Describe in around 100 words a character that is either: grieving, embarrassed or depressed. Or choose an emotion of your own. Tie it into your story outline if you wish.

Exercise 2

Imagine your character in a particular setting. Describe it using all of the senses. Again, use a scene from your story outline if you wish.

Exercise 3

Write a descriptive passage of an outdoor scene setting it two contrasting weather situations. Use a scene from your story outline if that is useful.

Exercise 4

Write two consecutive scenes which show a contrast in the characters' moods or the atmosphere of the scene. For example, a scene where everything is going right followed by a scene where it is all going horribly wrong.

Exercise 5

As an exercise think of an object. Now describe it using the relevant senses i.e. what you might see when looking at it; what sounds it might make; what it tastes like; what it feels like; what it smells like. Ask a friend or relative to try and guess what you have described. Repeat the exercise until you are bored (or your friend is).

Tip

Always leave off writing when you know what you are saying – halfway through a sentence even. That way when you return to it, you'll be in mid flow straight away.

Chapter Thirteen:
Editing and re-writing

Step 34: Editing and polishing your work

Difficult though it may be to write your story or novel in the first place, the editing and re-writing of it is just as necessary – if not more so.

No writer should ever be satisfied with their first, second or even third drafts. Editing is what can turn good writing into great writing. That in turn can make the difference between an acceptance letter and a rejection slip. So be prepared to re-write your work time and again, honing and polishing until it shines.

However, knowing how to edit and improve your writing is something of a skill in itself. And unless you know what you are looking for, you may struggle to improve upon your initial writing.

It is a good idea to make a copy of your story to work on and keep your original draft. If nothing else you can compare your early draft to your honed and polished story. But on the other hand, if you make radical changes which you later regret, you still have your original draft to return to.

All writers have their own approach to writing and editing. Perhaps you have been re-writing and polishing as you have gone along. Even so, you will need to look again at your finished work, to double check that it is the very best you can do. Other writers prefer to just crack on with their story and not look back until it is finished. Only then do they start looking at how to edit and improve it. There is no right or wrong way. It is entirely up to you. However be sure that you do edit, polish and re-write. I doubt there is a writer born who can write something word-perfect at the very first attempt.

How to edit your story

After slaving away for weeks, months or even years, you finally type *The End.* Undoubtedly, you will heave a huge sigh of relief, and possibly that relief will be tinged with sadness that your involvement with your characters has come to an end.

But if you think your next step is to print the whole thing off, pop it into a padded envelope and send it winging its way to the nearest publisher, you are sadly mistaken. Do that and you can be sure it will come winging its way home even faster.

Definitely congratulate yourself on completing your story, whether it is a short story or a full-blown novel; it is quite an achievement and you should be proud of yourself. But do not think the hard bit is over.

Let it rest

Put your story aside for a while. You will be too close and too wound up in it to look impartially at it straight away. So let it slumber for a while, even if it is just a few days. Some writers believe in letting their work rest for months before returning to it with that critical eye.

Of course you will have your own way of editing, but here is one suggestion. After a decent break from it, read it from start to finish – with a notebook and pencil to hand to jot down anything you find that jars, or fails to make sense, or is badly written. Anything in fact that needs looking at. Be prepared to make changes and re-write sections if necessary. Careful and meticulous editing could make all the difference between getting your story accepted or rejected. After spending so much time already on it, you owe it to yourself to give it the best chance possible.

What is it all about?

Looking at your story with fresh eyes, look out for holes in the plot, unexplained events, inconsistencies, and loose ends not tied up. Ask yourself whether you believe in your story. Does the plot feel contrived? Have the characters led the way or have you as author pulled all the strings?

You *must* believe in your story, your characters and this whole make-believe world that you have created. Even fantasy needs to be utterly believable. If *you* do not believe in it, then no one else will either. If you find that you do not completely believe in your story, then ask yourself why not. What would make it more realistic to you? Then act upon this.

Look at your characters

Your characters are at the heart of your story, it would be nothing without them. Are they believable or are they wooden and not true to life? Have you brought them to life through movement, action, reaction, speech and emotion? Have you controlled their every thought, word and action or somewhere along the line have they taken over and surprised you with the things they have said and done? Ideally, that is what you should be expecting to find, that your characters have become so real, they have brought their role to life and you as the author have given them the leeway to carry on. Look to see if your key character has changed in some way from how they were at the start of the story. Have they learned something, or moved on in some way? It is important that they are not the same at the end of the story as at the beginning. Let your characters grow.

Listen to the dialogue

As you know, dialogue should give the impression of real speech – that is real speech with all the boring bits taken out. Check that you have not left any boring bits in. Make sure that every word of dialogue has earned the right to be there. Do not pad your story with irrelevant speech that adds nothing to the story. Cut out laborious dialogue if the reader already knows that information via the narrative. Your dialogue should always be adding something new and relevant to your story.

Is your story lacking in emotion and atmosphere?

As you read it, are you caught up with the emotions of your characters? If not, why not? Maybe their problems are not difficult enough – in which case a major re-think could be needed. Maybe you have not described scenes well enough. Remember to bring all the senses into play.

Look at the narrative

Look and listen to the voice of your story – the narration. Let it be in line with the story itself and its characters. Let the tone of the narrative be at one with the rest of the story. A love story does not require a cynical narrative; a thriller will not want a jovial approach. Keep the viewpoint of your main character close at hand when the narrative is written so that they go hand in hand. Be sure it is not you, the author who is narrating this story; get inside the head of the key character and think as they would think as you are writing.

Is there too much narrative? Have you narrated major scenes that should have been enacted 'live' before the reader's eyes to evoke their emotion? Do you need to re-write certain scenes to bring them to life? Have you painted a clear picture of the world these characters live in? Watch out for sentences that tell instead of show. If there is 'too much information' then start deleting. Similarly if there are purple passages, i.e. sections which slow the story down and are only there to show what a brilliant writer you are – then hit the delete key!

Point of view

Do we see the story unfolding through the eyes and heart of the protagonist – your main character? Be sure you have not flitted in and out of the heads of other characters unintentionally. Similarly with the tenses – have you been consistent?

Go through your story and write in whatever is lacking – or make a note of sections that need more work so you can return to re-write them after you have given them more thought.

Back to basics:

- Look for spelling mistakes and grammatical errors.

- Look at the presentation. Is it double spaced, is each paragraph indented (or as your market requires)?

- Check the punctuation around dialogue. Have you got it perfect? And is it perfect consistently?

- Look for exclamation marks, and if you find any anywhere except in your dialogue (short bursts of dialogue preferably) delete them.

- Have you started a new paragraph with each character change – dialogue or action?

- Look out for excessive adjectives and adverbs.

Words of Wisdom

"When you think you've finished, put it to one side for a minimum of three weeks. Don't look at it, try not to even think of it. Then reread it. Then tell yourself you have been told by a publisher to cut an unfeasibly large proportion – say ten per cent. And do it. Then read it to yourself OUT LOUD. Always remember that the only person who knows that something has been cut out is YOU. However much you love a particular bit, it will not be missed."
Jan Needle

Exercise 1

Select what you feel is your best piece of writing so far. Edit it closely using the points outlined above.

Exercise 2

Apply the same editing and polishing process to other pieces of work you have written and intend continuing with.

Exercise 3

Look at your storyline created from the exercises in chapter 9 and try to polish this outline by adding further scenes, making the plot more detailed as well as building up more flesh around the skeleton.

Exercise 4

If you have not already written your opening scene to this story outline, time now to have a go. Remember to start where there is a change to the 'norm', where there is something different happening. Recap by re-reading Step 25.

Exercise 5

Look at what you have written and see if you can improve on it at this stage. When you are fairly happy with your work, move onto the next scene.

Tip

As you struggle to edit your work and find it unbearable to attack your manuscript so brutally, remember that in ancient Rome, 'editor' was the name given to the sponsor of gladiatorial combats. Today, it's still the job of the editor is to keep his audience happy and satisfied through the skilful application of cutting and slashing.

Chapter Fourteen:
Inspiration

Step 35: The creative mood

We might have the know-how to write, but we are not always in the mood. However, if you sit waiting for inspiration to strike you could be waiting forever. So when you sit down to write, do just that – write! The creative mood, if it is there at all can be snatched away at the drop of a hat or the slightest interruption. So try not to be a slave to your creative moods. Learn to treat writing as a job. A bricklayer is hardly going to stop laying his bricks just because the mood has gone; and a teacher will hopefully not clam up in class because she is no longer in the mood for teaching. Never mind if you are not in a creative mood, just knuckle down and write.

Overcoming writers block

There are times when you are really struggling to write something but to no avail. Call it 'writer's block' if you wish. If you find yourself in that situation, have a few 'tricks' up your sleeve, to give yourself a kick-start.

- Reading an extract from a 'teach yourself' creative writing book often helps, so keep yours close at hand.

- Google some quotes from famous writers about 'writing'. It will show you are not alone.

- Try writing some 'throw away' poetry. Not poetry to keep, but to simply throw away or delete.

- Try some 'free-style' writing. Simply pick random words from the dictionary and write about them without thinking.

Do not be too hard on yourself. You are after all trying to conjure something up from nothing, which is an amazing thing if you think about it.

The Writing Bug

If you have got the 'writing bug' then you are probably eager to start writing a novel. It is what most writers seem to aspire to. But remember – do not run before you can walk.

Writing a novel is a massive task, so be sure you are confident and skilled in all the many aspects of writing fiction before setting out on something huge. You need to understand about viewpoint, tense, conflict, characterisation, dialogue, flashbacks etc. And if there is anything you still are not sure of then study until you have totally grasped it. Then you will be able to concentrate on the important thing – the story.

Writing a novel is time consuming, so be sure that the story you have in mind is one that you are passionate about and feel absolutely dedicated to putting in the time and effort that will be needed to complete it.

Be aware that you will have to do a lot of planning beforehand; a lot of 'note writing' so that you can visualise the setting and understand the background and reasoning of your characters – all of them. You will probably have to do some research – fictional characters have jobs, hobbies, ailments, skills etc., be sure you don't make mistakes when you write about these because your mistakes will be quickly picked up by others in the know.

It is easy to get 'bogged down' with everything when writing a novel, so try and plan a skeleton outline of your story, (even though it may change). This way at least you should not write yourself into a corner.

Reminders:

- If you can envisage the scenes throughout your story, and recognize them as milestones in the journey, you will have targets to aim for.

- Write character sketches so that you know *everything* about them – even though you probably will not use a fraction of it in your story.

- Your characters must be facing a problem – emotional or physical, or both. Make this conflict real to them and do not let them get out of the difficulties easily. Basically, give them something to aim for which means the world to them, and then put every kind of obstacle in their path.

- Dialogue must be there for a reason. Make every word count.

- Flashbacks should be kept to a minimum. The reader wants to know what is going to happen more than they want to know what has happened.

Step 36: Know the path you are taking

Do not simply start your writing and allow it to wander this way or that way and see where it ends up. *Know* what you are writing. It does not *have* to fit under a specific genre, but it will help you to know whether you are writing a short story or a novel and whether it is a romance, a crime story, a thriller, a teenage book, a sci-fi story or whatever.

There are a multitude of themes and genres that you can write for so try and be clear in your own mind as to what you are writing. Know whether you are writing a thriller, or a science fiction story, or a humorous story, or a horror story, or an historical novel. Know if the story you are writing is your autobiography, or your family history. Is it a poem, an article, flash fiction, a short story, a novella or a novel? It might be a combination of genres, that is fine, so long as you know what you are doing. You, as the writer should be perfectly clearly in your own mind what you are writing. Have your goal in mind and know where you are going with it.

Romance for example: There are different levels of romance ranging from the erotic to the sentimental and from historic to contemporary. There will be a big difference in your readership if you are planning an erotic novel as opposed to a sentimental romantic magazine story. In both cases though you should understand what the reader wants from a story. You will find that out by reading stories that are already published within these markets.

Many people want to write for children. However some people choose to try writing for children thinking it is easier than writing for the adult market. In fact nothing could be further from the truth. The children's genre is a very discerning area and competition is high. So if you are thinking this is an easier route to take you will be sorely disappointed.

Step 37: Writing children's fiction

When it comes to children's fiction you definitely need to know your target age range and reading ability. Make sure the storyline is right for readers of that age and you have written the story with them in mind. Also be sure that the subject matter, vocabulary and sentence structure are suitable for that particular age group.

Books for babies

These are usually made from thick board or a waterproof, chewable plastic. They might have lift up flaps and be textured and quirky. The illustrations will be bright, simplistic and clear, while the text – if any, will be very sparse – maybe just a handful of words.

Books for toddlers

These books will often be read to them by a grown up. So again, lots of colourful illustrations which will keep them occupied even if an adult is not reading to them. However the text can be quite sophisticated with repetitions, lively phrases and colourful exciting words. These books are meant to be read aloud so lots of sections where junior can join in. If you are tempted to write rhyming prose, be aware that many publishers are not so keen because rhyming verse does not translate well – and publishers tend to think on a global scale.

Early readers

Here, you are looking at stories for children aged around 5-6 years who are just starting to learn how to read. So simple basic words and simple sentences are required but also a captivating story that will encourage them to read more.

Stories for 7-9 year olds

While these children may be able to read almost all the everyday words you put into your stories they might not always understand the meaning of some of them. Of course this is not a bad thing as it extends their vocabulary, however you do not want the text to be so tricky that it stops the flow of the story and discourages them. As for the story itself, children of this age are interested in everything from magic and dragons to ponies and elves. They love adventure and mystery – and stories that deal with everyday life from trips to the dentist to moving house and everything in between.

Stories for 9-12 year olds

The same can be said for readers of this age, but now the stories can be longer, more intriguing, more suspenseful. These children need stories that are going to hold their attention, so lots of action, adventure, emotion and great characters.

Stories for teens or young adult (YA)

Generally you can assume that children aged 13 and above are competent readers. They will pretty much understand the meaning of words as well as an adult. However they are not adults and this should be reflected in the writing of the stories, the theme, plot and the choice of words. At this age they are inquisitive about everything to do with growing up, so story content could include everyday issues that concern teenagers – anything from sex and bullying to love and grief, and lots more besides. They do also like fantasy, romance, horror, adventure. So plenty of scope here!

Hi-Lo stories

These stories or books are aimed at older children who have a much lower reading age. Imagine a child of 13 who only has the reading ability of a five year old. A great deal of skill is required in crafting out a story that will really interest him and encourage him to read more, yet with vocabulary and structure which is as simplistic as in a book for a much younger child.

Illustrations for children's books

You will not be expected to supply the illustrations for children's books. Publishers have their own stable of illustrators who they call on to provide the pictures. However if you are an artist first and foremost, then this should be established with potential publishers when first submitting your ideas or your manuscript. If a publisher or editor is interested they will guide you as to what illustrations are required and how they should be submitted. So it is probably best to just do sample illustrations for your book, rather than the entire artwork for the story, as editors tend to have their own ideas.

Words of Wisdom

"It is inevitable that one day you'll get up and not have a clue about what to write next. My solution to writers block is to have a few different writing projects on the go at any one time. If you're writing a book, have a couple of short stories or magazine articles on the go at the same time. If you're struggling with one of them, switch to writing something else for an hour or two. Soon, your creative juices will be completely restored and you'll be raring to get on with your main project again."
Michael Boxwell

Exercise 1

Free-style writing is a good way to get you into the writing mood if you are struggling with writers' block. This exercise is also an exercise in trusting yourself and developing your own style. So, think of a house, or a room in the house. Now bring it to life in no more than 200 words.

Exercise 2

Write 300 words on a particular season of the year – do not say what the season is, let your words paint the picture.

Exercise 3

As an exercise in writing for different age groups, write the following scene twice. Firstly so that it suits a five year old child who is just starting to read by himself, and then to suit a 12 year old reader. Scenario: *Jack is walking through thick mud and his boots become stuck.*

Exercise 4

Try writing this scene for a toddler (mum is reading it to them, but they are following the story) and a young adult (a 15 year old). Scenario: *Sally is in the park contemplating going on the swings and slides.*

Exercise 5

From the exercises above, select Jack or Sally (at the ages you prefer) and write a scene of mainly dialogue between them.

Tip

If you plan on making a duplicate copy of your story to edit, changing the font on the story you are editing will give a slightly different appearance and will help you look at it with a fresh perspective, so flaws and mistakes will show up more clearly.

Chapter Fifteen:
Writing short stories

Step 38: The short story

Some say the market for short stories is diminishing, however if you look at the many popular magazines on the newsagents' shelves you will find that there are still lots which regularly publish short stories, not to mention online publications. So do your market research and discover the publications that seem right for you.

The length of a short story varies from around 700 words to 7 or 8,000 words. Shorter than 700 and it is classed as flash fiction. A story of around 2,250 words would fit into a 15-minute radio short story slot. In general, magazine stories range from around 1,000 – 3,000 words. But if you have a publication in mind, check the word length they prefer and stick to it. Many journals offer fiction guidelines.

If you want to write short stories my advice is to read as many as you can. For a particular market, study published stories to get a feel for the style and content. Get to know what different publications like and what they publish. Look to see the usual number of characters involved in an typical story and whether they are usually written from one viewpoint or more. Ask yourself do they have a 'twist in the tale'? Look at the age range of characters and their lifestyles. Usually when a magazine has been printing a certain type of short story for years and it is still popular, they are not looking for change. So there is little point in trying to break the mould with a story that is totally alien to their usual style.

Short story competitions might provide a wider scope for your work, so keep your eyes peeled for such competitions. There are always lots about and prize money can be well worth winning, not to mention the esteem of being placed in a competition and what that does for your morale. Read the rules meticulously and stick to them.

There is an art in writing the short story. You have to get such a lot in within a relatively few number of words. You have to open with a 'punch', grab the reader at once, set the scene, establish the conflict, show the personality of the character and get the reader to immediately care that they have got a problem. Phew!

Usually (but not always) short stories are written with a single viewpoint – the story is told through the eyes and feelings of your protagonist. You need a strong storyline or plot, there is no time to meander aimlessly, the reader wants to know what is happening here and now. Nevertheless, you must write the story in a way that it is a pleasure to read. Your words must paint a picture, reflect the mood. It should flow. It should almost appear easy – when in fact you will have worked very hard to achieve that ease of reading. So much in such a short space of time!

So, what does a short story comprise of? Well it needs:

An original idea

A tall order to start with and you would be forgiven for thinking that there are no original ideas left under the sun. Except *you* are an original, and your writing is unique to you, so put your individual stamp on an idea and create something fresh and new. Be sure however that the idea excites you. Otherwise it's not going to excite anyone else either.

Believable characters

The short story revolves around its characters, so let your protagonist's problem be established straight away. Reveal the conflict they are facing by writing the story through their viewpoint. Use dialogue to reveal personalities and moods as well as to carry the story forward, but make sure that every word of that dialogue is there for a purpose.

A realistic setting

When writing to the restrictions of a word count, the luxury of rambling descriptions and narrative is not an option. Find ways of revealing the background by your succinct writing. Nevertheless you must still set the scene convincingly to engage your readers.

An intriguing beginning

Begin with the action in full flow. Set the scene, introduce the character and establish the conflict. Aim to grab the reader immediately and keep the story moving forward by ensuring there are no wasted words or unnecessary scenes or dialogue.

Conflict

Whether the conflict your protagonist is facing is physical or emotional, or both, let it be clear what he/she is up against. Get your reader on side with your main character, so they are rooting from the very start for him/her to achieve their goal.

Suspense

I am not suggesting breathtaking drama and heart-racing action, the suspense can be the anxiety or turmoil in the protagonist's mind. But be sure to have the suspense of the reader not knowing what your character is going to do to get through their difficulties and keep the momentum going.

Structure

The beginning, where you introduce your characters (not too many); set the scene and indicate the conflict. The middle, where the action develops with ever increasing interest. And the end where we see the problem resolved one way or the other. Keep the time span short, and avoid extending your story to an anti-climax with the tying up of loose ends. Ensure loose ends are all resolved before the climax.

A satisfying ending

Happy endings are not compulsory – although your market research may show otherwise. In any case make sure your ending leaves the reader satisfied and not left feeling puzzled or cheated. An unexpected (but totally believable) ending is always good.

Words of Wisdom

"Procrastination is nature's way of making sure you do not start writing until you are ready. It is also nature's way of making sure the floor gets mopped. I actually find these procrastination jobs are useful for thinking. Amazing how inspiring the skirting boards can be sometimes!"

Jackie Marchant.

Exercise 1

Research the market place (magazines and on-line magazines) which accept short stories. Study the market and note down possible outlets for your short stories. Look to see which are paying markets and avoid any where they expect you to pay them. See what short story competitions you can find – note the closing date however and read the rules carefully.

Exercise 2

Looking back at your early ideas (or come up with something brand new), sketch out a skeleton plot or outline for a short story for a publication/competition which appeals to you. (Look back at chapter 9 to recap on structure).

Exercise 3

Write a character sketch for you main character. (Refer back to chapter 7 to remind you about characters).

Exercise 4

Write the opening few paragraphs and see if you have started with a punch that will immediately grab the reader.

Exercise 5

Write your story, then re-write, edit and polish until it shines. Send it off. Chapter 18 provides advice on submitting your work to editors and publishers.

Tip

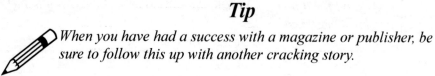 *When you have had a success with a magazine or publisher, be sure to follow this up with another cracking story.*

Chapter Sixteen: Writing about yourself

Step 39: Writing your autobiography

Lots of people think about writing their own life story, many have successfully done so. A great many autobiographies become best sellers – and they are not all written by celebrities. Many are written by ordinary people who have lived remarkable lives.

If you plan on writing your life story then I would suggest you browse the autobiographies in the library. See how they are crafted. See what makes them interesting and readable.

When planning your story, my advice would be to lightly plot it, so that you do not get completely bogged down with a lifetime's activities, achievements and conversations. Pick out the highlights, the low spots, the joyous and the sorrowful times. Let your mind slip back to occasions that you can remember vividly so you can write them with colour and emotion and really paint a picture of that moment in time for others to see.

While you may intend writing it in chronological order, your mind may have other ideas. Incidents and conversations will probably be popping up in your head at the least convenient time, so be sure to have notebooks at the ready to jot down your thoughts. If you are writing about one period of time and your thoughts suddenly jump forward a decade or two then write it as it occurs to you. Those thoughts may never come back as vividly. Note the change of time and place, log it down and find your own way of keeping track. Coloured pens may help or different fonts and indexed asterisks. This is certainly one style of book that is not straight forward.

However, like any book, it must be written in a way that engages the reader and interests them enough to keep reading. Vary the emotion, a happy scene might follow a sad scene or vice versa. It is doubtful you will recall actual conversations, but dialogue will bring your book to life, just as in any fictional book. Besides the reader may lose interest in a book that is purely narrated from start to finish.

Within this book, there will also have to be a biography about you, explaining who you are. This prologue might also give your reasons for writing your story.

Be aware that it probably will not be easy to find a publisher. However that applies to every form of writing. Getting published is difficult, the competition is great. You have to persevere, be aware of who publishes what; write your story as best you can and present it in a professional manner. And persevere! Don't give up. Develop a rhino hide to cope with the rejections. However read the rejections carefully and improve your work if they all seem to be indicating this.

Be aware too that there are other options to conventional publishers such as print on demand and ebooks, which we look at later in this guide. Beware however of vanity publishing. That is something you really do not want to get involved with – we take a closer look at that in the following chapter.

Step 40: Writing your family history

Writing your family history is a wonderful legacy for your family, relatives and descendants as well as being a fascinating project to embark upon. It is also a huge task to attempt, the very thought of which may daunt you from even beginning. However if you take it step by step, you will find the path easier.

Visualise your book

Ask yourself how you visualise your completed family history? Will it be a simple photocopied booklet to give to family members, or a full scale professionally published book. If the latter is your choice, unless you have an amazing family saga to tell, and the ability to write it in a way that publishers will be fighting over it, you probably will not find a publisher willing to take it on. Mid-way between the two, you could look at self publication, but get lots of quotes from printers beforehand and find out exactly what you are getting for your money. Avoid those vanity publishers at all costs.

Alternatively you could create a simple website and publish your anecdotes and family photos there. There are free websites available – browse the internet and see what suits you. Then let your family and relatives know the website address and they can view your hard work and research, and print off their own copy if they want to – at no cost to you at all.

What format?

Depending on the material you have to work with, decide on the format of your book. If you have lots of photographs, then you might want to plan your story as a gallery of images mingled with text as you write the stories and anecdotes that are associated with the pictures. Maybe the material you have are old diaries and letters, so you might plan to publish these along with your narrative to set the scene.

Scope

Decide upon the scope of your story. You might want to begin with the earliest known ancestor and follow him/her down through a single line of descent to present day. You could devote each chapter – or website page to each ancestor or each generation or line of descent. Alternatively you might want to start with the present day and work back in time. But again, plot your chapters/pages accordingly and have a plan so that it does not become too confusing and overlapped.

Research

You want readers to enjoy your family history so try not to make it just a dull list of dates and names. Your readers need to experience these people's lives. So find out what their daily lives must have been like through research. Even if you cannot find exact details of individual ancestors, you will be able to find out what was going on at the time in history, maybe even weather conditions if you can find freak storms or hottest summers recorded. You should be able to find out what living conditions were like, cost of foods, what was available and what was not – all kinds of things to bring your story to life.

So look at the political scene at the time; look at time-lines for major events such as wars, epidemics, disasters which may have had an influence at the time. Look at fashions, food, modes of transport, entertainment of the day. Research your ancestors' occupations so you can describe what their day to day life was like. Interview living relatives to get their personal memories and so add colour to your story.

Plot and theme

You might choose to give your story a plot and theme. Maybe it's a rags to riches story or a tale of survival against the odds. You might discover that your family crosses from one country to another in search of a better life. Or maybe your story is based around a family trade. Just like fictional stories, family history stories need a plot and theme too.

Starting point

Your story does not have to start at the earliest or most recent point. You could choose an interesting fact or story about an ancestor and begin your narrative with that. As in all works of fiction, you still need to grab your reader and captivate them until the end.

Exercise 1

Even if you have no plans to write and publish your autobiography, as an exercise write a list of the highlights you would cover if you were writing such a book.

Exercise 2

Consider whether you would write it in a chronological order, i.e. starting from your early memories and going forward; or starting at some other point in your life and using flashbacks.

Exercise 3

Think of a happy time in your life, and write this up, bringing as much colour and emotion as you can.

Exercise 4

Consider another important time in your life, and write this up too.

Exercise 5

Think of a humorous incident in your life and write this.

Tip

Remember that additional research will be needed even though it's your story, so do not rely on memory when writing about established facts.

Chapter Seventeen:
Beyond books

There is more to fiction than just writing books. TV, radio, plays and film all require writers; and there are courses and books to study from for every type of writing which will go into depth far greater than is possible to do in this guide. My advice is to read as many 'how to' books as you can; look at the BBC website for guidance; read the *Writers and Artists Yearbook* to gather more knowledge and immerse yourself in the particular genre that interests you. Once you have the solid foundations and know-how for writing fiction and non-fiction, and your presentation techniques are second nature, there is nothing to stop you from progressing in any direction you wish.

There are some great 'how to' books available on writing for radio. However, for this book I have decided to just touch on the subject here as a basic guide, because getting your work broadcast on radio is a real possibility for a writer who wishes to take that course. Here are a few brief notes to whet your appetite.

Step 41: Writing for radio

There are radio plays, radio short stories, radio talks and radio features. You will find radio at all levels, international, national, regional, community, hospital and college level. It is necessary however to listen to what they broadcast, and see where you could fit in.

Radio writing expert Vincent McInerney describes radio as a 'dragon constantly in need of food'. Radio is always going to be in need of good new material to broadcast. So it is definitely worth your while in considering this medium for your work.

You will find lots of information about writing for radio by looking at the BBC Writers Room website for guidance. They have sample scripts which will help you with the correct layout plus stacks of advice. (www.bbc.co.uk/writersroom)

Whether you want to write for radio or TV, the BBC Writers Room is where your script should be sent. They state that they read all unsolicited scripts for BBC films, TV drama, children's drama, TV comedy, radio entertainment and radio drama; and that they accept unsolicited scripts written for film, television, radio or stage.

Formatting your script properly helps. It suggests a professional approach to your writing; it is easier to read, assess and ultimately use; and most importantly, it can help you write to a particular format, and to think and write in visual terms. You can check out their Script Archive for examples of produced scripts.

And here is what happens to your script: The BBC Writers' Room employs experienced readers to assess unsolicited scripts and competition entries. The readers sift unsolicited scripts by reading the first ten pages. If a script hooks their attention, it will then be given a full read and the writer will receive feedback. If a script does not make it past the sift stage, then it gets returned to the writer without feedback.

They say they do not work to quotas – their readers are briefed to look for writing quality regardless of content, subject, message, setting, or writing experience. All scripts that have been given a full read are discussed during open, consultative feedback sessions.

They add also that they are unable to enter into further discussion about individual scripts, or about their reader's assessment, unless they decide to develop their relationship with a writer.

There are sometimes competitions for radio – and television, so keep yourself informed on what is happening within these worlds.

Step 42: Writing for the stage

As I have never had a West End stage play produced, I would not dream of trying to advise anyone on how to go about this – apart from reading the advice in the good old *Writers & Artists Yearbook* and other specialised books on the subject.

What I would point out that there are lots of amateur dramatic societies around who might welcome a brand new play to put on. You could also look to schools and colleges, even primary schools might welcome your adaptation of a seasonal play for their children to act out in assembly. You never know what doors will open to you unless you try. Look around at your own locality and see what possibilities are on hand.

My own experience in playwriting came just this way. When my children were in primary school I got together with some other parents and wrote, directed and produced a Christmas pantomime which we put on over a number of nights for the whole parish. It raised money for the school and was so successful – and such fun, that we put on five more pantomimes over the next five years. This gave me the confidence to write a short script for an educational video for a particular charity when the opportunity arose.

My advice to budding playwrights would be to learn how to lay out a script, see how actors and producers like to see the presentation and ensure your work fits that criteria. As always, give yourself the best possible chance to be up there in the running.

Words of Wisdom

"If you begin to feel despairing, rejected, like a failure, remind yourself that every step forwards a human body takes begins as a fall. No piece of writing you create is ever wasted. Even if it isn't published, the act of writing it has added to your skill and experience. It's one more step on your journey."
Leila Rasheed.

Exercise 1

Using a sample of a published script, follow the format and create a scene that mirrors the way the professional playwright sets out their play.

Exercise 2

Take time to listen to some radio plays and short stories. Try and listen with an analytic ear, to work out why they are successful.

Exercise 3

Whenever you have the opportunity of seeing a stage play, watch it with a view to learning from it (as well as enjoying). Analyse what goes on in the different scenes. See how the playwright handles time lapses and scene changes. Take note of the ratio of dialogue to stage direction.

Exercise 4

Try and write a practice scene – or the whole story, suitable for radio. If you manage the whole story, then definitely try and get it accepted. With your practice scene or story, bear in mind that your words need to really capture the attention of the listener; paint a clear picture with your dialogue and narrative. Make the plot absorbing.

Exercise 5

As an exercise, select your favourite TV drama or soap, and try to write a scene or two using the established characters. You may find this is something you are good at and as such the BBC Writers' Room may be just waiting to see your scripts.

Tip

Reading your work aloud to yourself is the best way to hear if you have the rhyme and rhythm of each sentence correct.

Chapter Eighteen:
Think Professionally

Step 43: Presentation

Presentation is so important. After you have put so much effort into writing your story, do not let yourself down by presenting it to a publisher or editor in anything but a totally professional way.

Print off your manuscript on one side of A4 paper, double spaced with good margins all around. Choose an easy to read font such as Times Roman Numeral, font size 12 or 14. Number each page ideally with a word of your name, a word of the title and the page number: e.g. *Evans/Rampage/17*

Type up a covering page giving the title, number of words, your name, your address and contact details. Include a brief covering letter.

Hold it together with an elastic band or paper clip and send it in a sturdy envelope addressed to the correct person. It is perfectly acceptable to include a stamped addressed postcard for them to acknowledge receipt of your manuscript. Include return postage if you want your manuscript back.

Many publishers and magazines now accept manuscript submissions by email, when this is the case, look to see what format they prefer and be guided by that. However your finished manuscript should be no less perfectly presented.

Step 44: Approaching publishers and editors

It goes without saying that different publishers publish different types of books. Be sure to do your research before sending your manuscript off. Check out *The Writers & Artists Yearbook* and browse bookshops and libraries to see who is publishing what. Look at selected publishers' websites and see what they have published in the past and what they are currently publishing.

Publishing houses have various ways of working. Many only agree to look at manuscripts if they are submitted by a literary agent. Some prefer an enquiry letter first, others will look at a few chapters and a synopsis, and some may want to see the whole manuscript. Your research will determine how each likes to be approached, but be sure to write your preliminary letter with the utmost care.

Step 45: Writing the synopsis

Most publishers will ask for sample chapters and a synopsis and I have
yet to meet a writer who enjoys writing the synopsis. The problem is in
knowing how much to put in, and deciding what to leave out. And just
how long should a synopsis be anyway?

Basically a synopsis is summarising your novel in a few pages. This
might range from one or two to a dozen or more pages. Different
publishers have different requirements.

In your covering letter you should state the approximate length of your
book, and who you think the story will appeal to – particularly when
writing for children, be specific with the age group you are aiming for.
Give a brief account of yourself regarding your writing career (a sentence
or two – not your life story).

The synopsis should be as well written as your actual book, and should
flow equally as easily. It should tell the entire story, from beginning to end
including the dramatic high spots and cliff-hangers. It should portray the
intensity and flavour of your book and give an account of the main
characters, the conflict they face and what they stand to lose. Remember
to edit and polish your synopsis until it sparkles before sending it off.

Step 46: Beware of vanity publishing

Be very careful that you do not get coerced into going for vanity
publishing. This term is applied to a publisher who promises to publish
your book for X amount of pounds – which can run into thousands of
pounds. The publishing house certainly will not be advertising themselves
as vanity publishing, they will find other terms to describe their method of
work.

Quite recently I sent a story off to a publisher that I had not heard of
before. They responded favourably towards my book, it was going before
their board of editors, building my hopes up. When the news came that
their board liked it and wanted to publish, naturally I was delighted – until
they asked for almost £2,000 as my contribution towards publishing. My
next letter to them was thanks but no thanks.

So beware. Certainly these publishers will produce your book. The cover
(which may cost you extra) probably will look good; if you want it
professionally copy-edited that too will cost extra, most probably. If you

want them to market or do some promotion, it is more than likely that will also be added to your bill.

Pricing your vanity published book will have to be quite high if you are ever to recoup your losses, and this in turn will make it difficult for you to sell your book. Plus you might find it difficult to find bookshops willing to stock it.

Please beware. There are other ways of producing your book yourself if that is the course you want to take. Print on demand will cost you a fraction of the price. Locating a local printer will allow you to get a fair quote. Ebooks will not cost you a penny.

The big difference between being published by a mainstream publisher or self publishing is that an established publisher will proof read and copy edit your book, so that when it hits the shelves it is going to be word perfect. If you are self publishing, then you will have to do this yourself. And it is vital that you do. Do not skip this stage if you want your book to be something to be proud of. There are good proof reading and copy editing people out there who will give you a fair quote for undertaking work on your manuscript.

Step 47: Print on demand

There are numerous print on demand companies which you will find by browsing the internet. Please read their information thoroughly and work out precisely what the cost to you will be, and what exactly you get for your money.

Basically the main cost comes from the initial setting up of your text in the correct format and appearance, along with creating artwork for the front and back covers – and spine. You might be providing these yourself, or you might need the company to provide them for you. Once this is set you will be able to have as few or as many books printed upon demand as and when you wish at a minimal cost per book.

A reputable print on demand company should provide your book with an ISBN number (this International Standard Book Number is a unique number by which any book can be identified) and be linked into the various marketing outlets such as Amazon where your book can be viewed, bought and sent out to the purchaser.

Step 48: eBooks

Ebooks are digital books that can be bought on the internet from publishers' websites, bookshop websites and outlets such as Amazon and Smashwords etc. Buyers of these books download them either onto their PC, or digital reading devices such as iPad's and Kindles.

Producing your book or collection of short stories, poems, articles, autobiography, family history – or whatever, is an accessible way of getting your work on show. Beware however that it *will* be on show – including all your spelling and grammatical mistakes, the flaws in your plot, bad dialogue and characterisation – if you allow those to slip through.

So while you might be excited about the prospect of producing your work as an ebook do not rush and overlook the vital elements of making your work word perfect and a great read. The website where your book can be obtained invites customer reviews, and the last thing you want is a pile of reviews from disgruntled customers complaining about the faults and failings of your book.

With that point drummed home, when your story has reached the final stage of turning a manuscript into ebook format, you will find reformatting your text for reading digitally quite different from when you are submitting to a publisher.

Bearing in mind it could be read on someone's phone, you need it single spaced, and avoid lots of white space between scene changes. You do not need page breaks except when there is a new chapter. You will also need to write the copyright small print at the start of your book. And remember at the end to write a little bit about the author. It is a good place to direct readers to your website or other books you have written.

Be prepared to work at getting the formatting exactly right. You will be able to view how it looks on a 'reader' as you upload. Be prepared to spend time getting your book to look just right and you may have to re-load your ebook text a number of times before being completely happy with the layout.

Prior to this, you will need to have worked out the price you want to sell your book at, and written the blurb, including 'ad words' in your book description which will be picked up by people browsing for this type of book. There is a superb book by Mike Boxwell called *Make an EBook* which takes you step by step through the process. I would heartily recommend you read that for step by step advice and instruction.

Step 49: The roll of the literary agent

Literary agents work with authors and publishers to get their clients' books published at the best possible terms. Authors do not pay their agents – the agent's fee comes when a publisher buys an author's work, then the agent gets their 10%, 15% or 20% (whatever has been agreed).

You do not need a literary agent to get published. The benefit of having an agent is because publishers value their opinion, and know that if a manuscript has come via an established agent it will be to a certain standard and may be right for them.

Getting a literary agent is not easy. Agents earn their money through you, the author, so you need to be a 'viable proposition' for an agent to be willing to take you on. You can find a list of literary agents in *The Writers & Artists Yearbook*, and your first point of contact would be via an enquiry letter or email to see whether they would be interested in looking at your book with a view to representing you.

Step 50: Coping with rejection

Every published writer will have had rejections at some time or other. Many great novels have struggled to find a publisher to begin with and then gone on to become household names. So do not let the fear of rejection put you off writing or make you afraid to send your work out.

Be aware that rejection happens. Pre-warn yourself that you will handle it when it does – and that it will make you all the more determined to succeed. However you can lessen the chances of rejection if your work is well written, that your presentation is excellent and you have sent it to an appropriate magazine or publisher. You can also increase your chances of success by having lots of work out looking for publishers at any one time.

When you receive a rejection letter, read it thoroughly, and if it offers any advice then take it to heart and learn from it. Do not feel bitterly disappointed and think you are a failure. Just look again at your manuscript, see if improvements can be made and then send it winging its way to another appropriate publisher.

Words of Wisdom

"Do not let rejection make you give up! I have found it useful to read parts of a new story to two writing friends – and they do the same – friendly criticism often helps. If any agent/publisher says anything helpful – take note! I have had many ups and downs over a very long writing career but managed to publish 30 books, with a lot of blood, sweat and tears!"
Griselda Gifford.

Exercise 1

Working from your story outline created in Chapter 9 (or a story of your choice), write a synopsis as if you were intending to submit it to a publisher.

Exercise 2

Hone and polish this synopsis so it sparkles and is all set to attract a publisher.

Exercise 3

Imagine you have been successful with this book. Now you have been asked to write the short blurb that goes on the back of the book. Make it so good that readers will want to buy it.

Exercise 4

Here is a possible start to a new story, see what you can do with it.
Scenario: *Her book manuscript had been at the publishers for three and a half months, but now she stared at the bulky brown envelope the postman had just delivered...*

Exercise 5

And another scenario to keep you going, although by now I hope you are bursting with ideas. Scenario: *It was the weirdest thing he had seen in his life...*

Tip

 Remember, if there is one trait that a writer needs to develop on top of all his or her creative skills, it is PERSEVERANCE.

Good luck with your writing.

Ann Evans

Please visit my website: www.annevansbooks.co.uk

Thank you for buying this book, I hope you have found it useful and that it will provide a good foundation for your writing.

Another exercise! Write a review of this book for Amazon, or email to me at: ann-evans@btconnect.com

Acknowledgements

I would like to thank the following authors for their generosity in providing the 'Words of Wisdom' in this book. Thank you so much...

Susan Jane Smith, B.Sc.
www.EmotionalHealthForEmotionalWealth.co.uk

Karen King. www.KarenKing.net

Roz Morris. www.NailYourNovel.com and
www.RozMorris.WordPress.com_

Simon Cheshire. www.SimonCheshire.co.uk

Rosalie Warren. www.Rosalie-Warren.co.uk

Bill Kirton. www.Bill-Kirton.co.uk

Andy Seed. www.AndySeed.com

Dan Holloway. www.EightCuts.com

Joan Lennon. www.JoanLennon.co.uk

Jan Needle. www.JanNeedle.com

Jackie Marchant. www.JackieMarchant.com

Cally Phillips. www.CallyPhillips.WordPress.com

Leila Rasheed. www.LeilaRasheed.com

Griselda Gifford. www.Griselda.co.uk

Michael Boxwell. www.MakeAnEbook.org

Recommended Further Reading

The Writers and Artists Yearbook

The Children's Writers and Artists Yearbook

On Writing by Stephen King

Get your Articles Published by Lesley Brown and Ann Gawthorpe

The Craft of Writing Articles by Gordon Wells

The Writing Business by Liz Taylor

Writing for Cash by John Atkinson and Beryl Sandwell

Writing for Children and Teenagers by Lee Wyndham

Writing for Radio by Vincent McInerney

Make an EBook by Michael Boxwell

Useful Websites

The Society of Authors: www.SocietyOfAuthors.org

Society of Editors and proofreaders: www.sfep.org.uk

Public Lending Right: www.plr.uk.com

Personal Recommendations

Tysall's Photography for covers and publicity shots – www.TysallsPhotography.org.uk

Greenstream Publishing is a friendly, approachable, thoroughly professional publisher who provides high quality books that inform, educate and excite their readers – www.GreenstreamPublishing.com

Andres Alzate is an illustrator and graphic designer with a quirky, clear style full of personality and humour. Originally from South America he now lives in England – AndresAlzate.DeviantArt.com

Naomi King creates illustrations and accessories based on the natural world – www.nemki.co.uk

For a professional editing service at very reasonable prices, visit www.SheilaGlasbeyBookEditing.weebly.com

About the Author

Ann Evans is a self-taught writer. Her writing career began over thirty years ago as a hobby. It was a hobby that became a career and a way of life. She was born and bred in Coventry, England, has three grown up children and four young grandchildren. She writes for children and adults in both fiction and non-fiction genres. She is often invited to give talks and workshops in schools and at literary events.

Ann says: "I discovered how to become a published writer through trial and error over many years. With the help and encouragement of family and friends, perseverance paid off, and a lifestyle involved in writing has become a reality. I love to be able to help others who are keen to write, and I hope this step by step guide will do just that."

Thank you for buying it.

Ann Evans books:

Cry Danger ISBN 0 590 13163 X Published 1995

Cry Danger ISBN 1 904 529313 (reprint)

Disaster Bay ISBN 0 590 19249 3 Published 1997

Deadly Hunter ISBN 0 590 19716 9 Published 1998

Fishing For Clues ISBN 0 439 01148 5 Published 2000

Stealing The Show ISBN 0 439 01208 2 Published 2000

Pushing His Luck ISBN 0 439 01149 3 Published 2000

The Beast ISBN 0 7460 60343 Published 2004

The Reawakening ISBN 0 746 07882X Published 2007

Rampage ISBN 978 0 7460 7892 1 Published 2008

Children's History of Coventry ISBN 978 1 84993 116 8

Look out for… A Touch of Death (Short story) in 13 Murder Mysteries (Scholastic). ISBN 0 590 13419 1996

A Tropical Affair (written as Ann Carroll)

Champagne Harvest (written as Ann Carroll)

British Customs (Teach Yourself) Brown Publishing. ISBN 1 873803 14 1 1993.

Britain and the British – General Topics. Brown Publishing ISBN 1 873803 03 6 1992

Index

Lightning Source UK Ltd.
Milton Keynes UK
UKOW052322171212

203802UK00008B/843/P